SURVIVAL GUIDE FOR THE UNDOCUMENTED IMMIGRANT

+ DACA, TPS, & VISA OVERSTAYER

IN TRUMP'S AMERICA

I0492635

Migration Research, LLC

LEGAL ADVICE DISCLAIMER

This book is presented solely for information purposes. The authors are not offering it as legal, case-specific, or other professional service advice. While the authors used best-efforts in preparing this book, they make no representations or warranties of any kind and assume no liabilities of any kind concerning the accuracy or completeness of the contents, and specifically disclaim any implied warranties for a purpose. Furthermore, because the information contained herein is considered timely, some or all of it is subject to change based on federal, state, or local law changes. The authors or publishers shall not be held liable for nor be responsible to any person or entity concerning any loss or incidental or consequential damages caused, or alleged to have been caused, directly or indirectly, by the information contained herein. No guarantees may be created or extended by sales representatives or written sales materials. Every immigration case is different, and the advice and strategies contained herein may not be suitable for your situation. You should seek the services of a competent professional about legal advice. This book is in no way associated with USCIS or any agency of the U.S. Government nor is it associated with any organizations mentioned herein.

**ATTENTION:
THE INFORMATION CONTAINED IN THIS BOOK IS AS OF
JUNE 2018. SOME RULES AND LAWS MAY CHANGE
WITHOUT NOTICE. WE WILL DO OUR BEST TO UPDATE
THE BOOK.**

A special thank you to all the valuable information from immigration websites and immigration organizations including USCIS and the U.S. Department of Justice. Furthermore, we would like to thank Chelsey Burden for copy editing and her relentless passion; Elliot Alford, Esq. for his useful input and support on the legal questions; Margarita Quezada and Alejandra Becerra for endless hours of translating and editing the Spanish version; Sandra Saltrese-Miller., Esq. for putting us on the path of immigration with her passionate love for law; Brand M., Esq. for his many edits on workers' rights; and the countless people we met along this nearly two-year journey including Kyler Mejia, Dieter & Irmgard Wiesemeyer in Germany.

Book Cover Artist: Enrique Felix, a wonderfully talented artist who resides in Tijuana, Mexico

Name of painting: Liberty in Crisis

Researched and written by Sabine and Andy Wiesemyer

Version: June 2018
1.1

ISBN-13: 978-1722483562
ISBN-10: 1722483563

Table of Contents

FORWARD

Welcome to the United States! The authors of this book firmly believe that you as well as the other 11+ million undocumented citizens of the world living in the United States are vital to the country's economic success. The United States is made up of immigrants from every country in the world along with millions of Indigenous people. What built this country is imagination, hard work, and dedication to success. However, the authors of this book know from personal experience how difficult the legal system can be for immigrants wanting to become documented (obtain a green card.) We hope this book will improve your chances so eventually, you can become documented and realize your dreams.

Today, in the era of President Trump, life in the United States as an undocumented person can be even more challenging. Sometimes laws are applied differently, and rules change when a different political party takes control. Under President Obama, **ICE** focused on undocumented criminals. However, today under Trump, as little as a traffic ticket from a broken taillight can get you deported — even if your only mistake was being in the country without documents.

President Trump has made a promise to his supporters to deport as many undocumented people as possible. He is doing everything in his power to change the rules, so he can make your life difficult. Trump is also trying to limit the ways you can become legal. This means the sooner you take action to become documented, the better your chances are.

Some people want to help you, others want to steal from you, and still, others want to deport you. You must be prepared for anything, learn to lay low, and be aware. The Trump administration will not last, nor will their policies. We want you to learn how to survive without being deported until you become legal or until Trump is gone and the rules surrounding immigration become reasonable.

This book does not and cannot provide legal advice. Only an Immigration Expert can do that.

The authors are not lawyers, nor do they represent themselves as such. Through extensive research and direct experience, this book was written to offer ideas and tips on how you can become legal. We will say this many times throughout the book: **hire a lawyer or accredited immigration consultant (Immigration Expert) to assist you. You can only receive advice from them. According to the American Immigration Lawyers Association, using an expert will improve your chances of becoming legal by as much as 70%.**

How to Use This Book

This book is designed to help you understand how to become legal and how to live and work in the United States. It's written in a simple, uncomplicated language for everyone. At the end of this book, you will find useful phone numbers, websites, definitions, and other resources.

The book will focus on how you arrived, your experience and actions while here, and what your chances are of becoming documented. It will also teach you how to be successful in your immigration application.

Step One: Read each suggestion and find the one that best describes your experience of how you arrived. Underline it and then move on to *Chapter Three*.

Step Two: In *Chapter Three*, read the sections that apply to you the most. It is good to review all the sections to see if more than one applies to you. Make a note of each that you think may work. There may be more than one possible path.

Step Three: Read *Chapter Four* and pay attention to what your story must contain for your application to be successful. Carefully recall your experience in your home country for an Asylum Application or learn how to prove hardship in a Family or Marriage Application.

Step Four: Read *Chapter Seven* and carefully select an Immigration Expert who can help you through the process.

This book can be your lifeline. It may make the difference between you living here in the United States or getting deported back to your home country. We designed it so that you can keep it with you. Memorize the important parts because if you get detained, Immigration Customs Enforcement (ICE) may take this book from you.

Get to know the icons:

 Important points to think about

 Important points to memorize

 Be careful! This could be dangerous

 Tasks you need to do

Be Prepared and Know Your Rights

This section is an overview of the most important points you must remember to survive in Trump's America. Even if you do not read the entire book, read this section to know what to do if detained by the local police or Immigration Customs Enforcement (ICE).

Regardless of whether you are an undocumented immigrant, visa overstayer, woman, man, or child, one thing you MUST know is that everyone has rights in the United States — including you. It is important that you express and protect your rights and have a plan if something happens to you or a family member.

You may have come from a country where the government is not well-established, where corruption is common, or where leaders have little respect for citizens. Being physically, mentally, or emotionally abused by your home country's leaders, police, or gangs could be the very reason you came here. In the United States, the laws are clear, and it is extremely important to know that if the police or anyone else harms you physically or attempts to extort money out of you, they can be arrested and charged with a crime.

A crime against you could also be a way of obtaining legal residency in the United States (U-Visa).

In the United States:
- ✓ Police and ICE cannot physically harm you (unless you are resisting arrest).
- ✓ Police and ICE cannot extort money from you or trade favors with you.
- ✓ You cannot bribe someone for a favor.

✓ Police, ICE, public officials, and lawyers do not have "special connections" that can help you, even if they say they do.

However, be aware that police and ICE will try to trick or intimidate you to gather evidence and deport you.

Corruption in the United States does occasionally happen, and when it does, you must have someone on your side who knows the laws and can help you. Don't let ICE, local police, or your employer intimidate you because you are undocumented. **Remember, you have rights.**

Be prepared in case you are detained.

Trump's goal is to deport everyone he possibly can. To ICE, you are only a number, and all they care about is deporting you back to your country as fast as possible even if your life may be in danger. In detention, they will put pressure on you to sign a deportation letter. Doing so makes their lives easy, but you end up on the next bus or plane to your birth country. If your life would be in danger if returned to your home country, **DON'T SIGN ANYTHING AND DO CLAIM ASYLUM**. Tell them you would like to talk to a lawyer (Immigration Expert). Your chances of becoming documented are much better if you use an Immigration Expert. **If you believe you have a legal reason to live in the United States, don't let them take that right away from you. However, if you only say you are here to make money, make a better life, or to be with your family, ICE will deport you.**

On the next few pages you will find a list of your rights as well as helpful tips to remember while living and working as an undocumented person in the United States.

What you must remember:

1) <u>**If ICE or the police are knocking on your door, NEVER give them permission to enter your home.**</u> DO NOT open the door unless they can give you a judge-signed warrant which they can show through a window or slide under the door. **The warrant MUST have your correct name, the correct address, and a signature by a judge** (this is one of your rights). Remember, **ICE will lie to you and play tricks**. Don't believe them and don't give them information about your immigration history (besides your name) unless they have a real warrant. Don't let them intimidate you. If you let them in your house and they ask you questions about your citizenship, they can arrest you. <u>**Always know who is on the other side of the door before you open it.**</u> If ICE agents break down your door without a real warrant, a good lawyer could use that against them, and you may be eligible for money. You need pictures, videos, and documentation of what happened. Read *Chapter Six* on being detained.

2) <u>**If the police approach you on the street, do not say anything.**</u> Do not admit you are undocumented but also do not lie. Unless you are within **100 miles** of the United States border and they have a reason to suspect you are doing something illegal, no one has the right to ask where you are from or if you are a citizen. If anyone asks, don't answer the question. Ask them if you are doing anything illegal. If they ask again, ignore their question and repeat, <u>**"Did I do anything illegal?"**</u> Then

say, **"May I go now?"** Keep asking these same questions. They must let you go unless you are doing something that is against the law. If they arrest you, ask them the reason (you have the right to know the reason). Read *Chapter Six* on being detained.

3) If the police arrest you for any reason, stay silent except to say, **"Please know that I have chosen to exercise my right to remain silent and I refuse to answer your questions. I request to contact my lawyer immediately."** However, do not lie to them about being a U.S. citizen because any lies will be used against you in court. Simply lying to them will give them what they need to deport you. If they ask where you are from, do not tell them. **Do not admit to or sign anything.** Believe us; they will try to make you talk. What they want is information they can use against you for deportation. Give them your name and tell them you would like to have your lawyer present when you answer any questions or sign any papers. Read *Chapter Six* on being detained.

4) If you are in detainment by the local police or ICE, ICE has 48 hours to initiate deportation proceedings or they must release you. Sometimes ICE may detain you for longer periods by placing a "hold" to give ICE more time to build their case. **In no way can ICE or the police hold you for more than 72 hours without ICE giving you a Notice to Appear (NTA).**

5) **To avoid expedited deportation, always carry something with you that proves you have been in the U.S. for at least two years.** If you are in proceedings,

you should carry a copy of any letters from United States Citizenship and Immigration Services (**USCIS**). Trump has been trying to expand expedited deportation (deportation without any legal defense), and if you cannot prove how long you have been here, they could deport you a few days after your arrest. If the police ask how long you have been in the United States, give them the proof. Proof can be a check stub, a bill, or a receipt with the date and your name on it. They can still detain you, but they cannot deport you. **Do not carry fake identification such as a fake social security card. Do not carry your country passport. Do not carry any documents with your current home address.**

6) **Develop a family backup plan including a POWER OF ATTORNEY**. Having a plan will save you problems if you or someone in your family is ever detained or deported. While living here, you may have purchased items such as a home or automobile, or perhaps you have children that may or may not be citizens. If deported, you should set aside money for when you are back in your home country. A notary or lawyer can help you complete the **Power of Attorney** form which will delegate some decision-making power to a person who you trust to protect your children and assets. In case you get detained, have an Immigration Expert available that already knows you. It is essential that you create a plan and be prepared. Read *Chapter Eight* on being prepared.

7) **Hire a lawyer or an Immigration Expert now.** Do not wait another moment. You want to have at least one consultation with an Immigration Expert. They can help you find out your chances of becoming legal, and you can call on them if you get detained. **If ICE detains you and you do not have someone you can call, finding an Immigration Expert is very difficult.** A notary cannot help you in court. They must be a lawyer or an accredited representative. Also, be aware that bad, greedy, and dishonest lawyers exist. Be sure to find a good lawyer and **find one before you need one.** Read *Chapter Seven* to learn more.

8) **Learn to lay low.** It is essential that you **learn not to do things that might bring attention to you**. For example, things like fighting or drunk-driving can get you detained and likely deported. Blending in will reduce your chances of being noticed and detained. See *Chapter Nine* on how to avoid ICE.

9) **Keep all legal, financial, and immigration documents in one place.** If you are detained or if you want to become legal, keeping all your papers in one place is very important. Your Immigration Expert will want to know how long you have been in the United States, what jobs you have had, and where you have lived. Having all your documents organized will make immigration proceedings go much faster. See *Chapter Eight* on being prepared.

IS ICE LOOKING FOR YOU?
HOW TO AVOID BEING DETAINED

If you have been detained and released by ICE, you have an **A-Number.** If you know it, call: 1-800-898-7180 to find out if you have a deportation order. If you don't know your **A-Number**, contact an Immigration Expert or a non-profit organization. They can help you find it. If you learn you have a deportation order, you MUST do the following:

- ✓ Use this book to learn about your options and then contact an Immigration Expert or non-profit organization working in immigration.

- ✓ Find a new place to live without your name on the lease. Do not have mail sent to the new home. There should be no public record of you living there.

- ✓ Go "off-grid." ICE uses electronic tracking methods to find you. Do not use credit cards. Pay cash for everything you do. Do not make any electronic transactions using your name and current address.

- ✓ Be sure that your car is not in your name or you have replaced your license plate in the last three years.

- ✓ If you are on social media such as Facebook, terminate your account or use a different name.

- ✓ If you must drive, be extra careful to not violate any laws. Make sure that your vehicle has up-to-date tags and that all parts are in working order.

- ✓ Keep in mind, most honest lawyers will not tell you to avoid a judge's order because it is unethical for them to say that.

Introduction

There are many reasons people come to the United States. It is often to seek a better life, but more recently it is to escape from the gangs and cartels which have taken over much of Mexico and Central America. It may also be to escape from being the victim of oppressive governments or extreme prejudice elsewhere in the world.

But, sadly, it is becoming less safe here as well. With Trump's ICE agents invading homes and businesses, the question that keeps many people awake at night is, "Because I am undocumented, is tomorrow the day I end up in the wrong place, get arrested, and end up deported?"

Your ability to become documented comes down to four questions:

Memorize

- ✓ **How did I enter?**
- ✓ **What is the reason I came to the United States?**
- ✓ **Have I been a good person while living in the United States?**
- ✓ **Do I have family who is legally here (spouse, parents, or children)?**

If you entered with a visa, the legalization process is much easier than if you entered without documentation. If you entered the country without documentation (no visa), it is difficult but not impossible. You have options.

<u>Chapter One</u>

How Did You Arrive in the United States?

"The bosom of America is open to receive not only the Opulent and respected Stranger but the oppressed and persecuted of all Nations and Religions; whom we shall welcome to a participation of all our rights and privileges…" –George Washington

----

What You Will Learn:

How did you arrive in the United States?
- ✓ **I am a visa overstayer**
- ✓ **I went to the border and officers released me into the United States**
- ✓ **I entered the United States without being caught; authorities do not know I am here**
- ✓ **I was never caught crossing the border, but now I am in deportation court proceedings**
- ✓ **I crossed the border without parents when I was under the age of 18**
- ✓ **I was brought to the United States against my will or under a false promise and was forced to work**

Words to Know:

Immigration Expert: We mean a lawyer or person authorized to provide immigration services by a state or federal government agency. We do NOT suggest notaries or others who are not authorized by a state or federal government.

Undocumented: A person who entered the United States without inspection (without an entry visa)

Overstayer: A person who entered the United States legally on a visa but stayed past the expiration date

TPS (Temporary Protected Status): A person who entered the United States with or without documentation and received a Temporary Protected Status due to a condition in their home country

DACA (Deferred Action for Childhood Arrivals): A person who was brought to the United States with or without inspection as a child (under 18) by a parent or legal guardian and who later applied for protection under the DACA program

Introduction

If you are in the United States without legal entry, becoming legal may be expensive and difficult. However, depending on your reasons, it is possible. How and when you originally entered will be relevant to your possible pathways to becoming documented.

Becoming legal depends on:
- ✓ Why you came to the United States in the first place
- ✓ Whether you have been a good person while you have been here
- ✓ What might happen to you if you were forced to return to your home country
- ✓ Whether you have a close family member who is a U.S. citizen
- ✓ Whether you find a good Immigration Expert

Your chances of obtaining a green card are not good if these apply to you:
- ✓ **Multiple Felonies:** If you have committed a felony or have been convicted of two or more serious misdemeanors (minor crimes), you would most likely be deported.
- ✓ **Multiple Re-entries:** If you re-entered multiple times without documentation after 1997, your chances of becoming documented are slim. Your second entry after being deported is considered a felony.
- ✓ **Terrorist Activity:** If you were accused of any act of terror anywhere in the world, your chances of becoming documented are slim.

✓ **Association with a Political Party That Promoted Terrorism:** If you were accused of being associated with a political party that promoted terrorist activities, your chances are slim. You would want to consult with an Immigration Expert to help explain your participation, as well as to see how your knowledge might assist the United States Government in fighting terrorist groups.

✓ **Making False Claims to an Immigration Officer or on an Immigration Form:** If you were caught making a false claim of being a U.S. citizen, or were caught putting down false information on an immigration form, your chances are slim. However, you may still be able to apply for asylum.

ATTENTION: If you fall into any of the above categories, we suggest you skip this chapter and go directly to *Chapter Three* and review **Defensive Asylum, Withholding of Removal, and CAT.** You need a good credible fear story. Also, read *Chapter Four* on developing your story. Once you have your story, contact an Immigration Expert.

If you are from **Nicaragua, Cuba, Guatemala, El Salvador, certain countries in Eastern Europe, or Haiti,** there may be a way for you to avoid deportation. In 1997, Congress passed two laws. Under these laws, certain people from the above countries could get lawful permanent resident status and stay in the United States. The requirements are different depending on your home country. If you are from one of these countries and have been here since 1997, speak to your Immigration Expert about the Nicaraguan Adjustment and **Central American Relief Act (NACARA)** or the **Haitian Refugee Immigration Fairness Act (HRIFA).** If you are the spouse or child of someone who qualifies for relief under these laws, you might also qualify.

LIFE Act: Under the Legal Immigration Family Equity (LIFE) Act, if you are the beneficiary of a visa petition or labor certification application that was filed between January 14, 1998 and April 30, 2001, you may be eligible for adjustment of status under Section 245(i). This means the beneficiary of the petition can become documented through Family Petition or Marriage Petition without leaving the country or asking for a waiver. You would have to pay a $1000 fine.

Requirements:
- ✓ You must have been present in the U.S. prior to December 21, 2000
- ✓ You must have been the beneficiary of an immigrant petition or labor certificate filed on or before April 30, 2001

NOTE: If your labor certificate or immigrant petition was approved before January 1998, you do not have to prove presence in the U.S. prior to December 21, 2000.

There are several things you must do to qualify. Again, contact an Immigration Expert to see if you qualify.

STEP ONE:
How Did You Arrive? Read each of the headings
in this chapter and select the one that best fits
how you arrived.

I am a Visa Overstayer

According to the Department of Homeland Security, 40% of the undocumented people living in the United States today came here legally with a visa. If you have stayed past your visa expiration date, the process to become legal is easier than if you came in undocumented (without a visa).

As an overstayer, **ICE** cannot deport you until a judge has determined that you are no longer legal to live and work in the United States. Technically, it is possible to live and work here until the day that someone turns you in and a judge makes a ruling. But, living in Trump's America, do you want to take that chance?

Options for Becoming Legal as a Visa Overstayer:

- ✓ **Marriage Petition with a U.S. Citizen:** You have a good chance of receiving a green card if you marry a U.S. Citizen. And, you will not have to return to your home country or show extreme hardship.

If your petitioner (spouse or family member) is a Green Card Holder, you are NOT immediately eligible to obtain a green card. Immigration Services limits the number of green cards issued to the beneficiary of a legal permanent resident. You must talk to an Immigration Expert to understand the process and waiting time. The process would be much easier if your petitioner became a citizen first.

- ✓ **Family Petition:** If you have an immediate family member who is a U.S. citizen or legal resident, they can petition for you. You will not have to go back to your home country or show extreme hardship. A U.S. citizen who is over the age of 21 can petition for:

- o Spouse
- o Children, unmarried and under the age of 21
- o Parents
- o Brothers and sisters

✓ **Battered Spouse (VAWA, U-Visa):** This applies to both women and men. You came here on a visa and married a U.S. Citizen or Green Card Holder. If your spouse emotionally or physically harmed you or held you against your will, you could apply for a U-Visa without them knowing.

✓ **Victim of Trafficking (T-Visa):** You were brought here with the expectation of visiting or a job opportunity but were forced into the sex industry or other forced labor. You may be able to apply for a T-Visa. **See *Qualifying Crimes* at the end of this book for a full list of what qualifies.**

✓ **Victim of a Crime in the United States (U-Visa):** While you were here, you were a victim of a crime. For example, you were robbed, physically assaulted, raped, extorted, or beaten. If you reported the crime to the police, you might be eligible for a U-Visa. **See *Qualifying Crimes* at the end of this book for a full list of what qualifies.**

✓ **Fear for Life If Returned Home (Asylum):** If you can explain that your life would be in danger if returned to your home country, you could qualify. You would apply for "**Affirmative Asylum.**"

✓ **Ten-Year Cancellation of Removal:** This is also known as the "42-B." **You must have lived in the United States for more than ten years without leaving the country.** You will have to be in deportation court proceedings to apply. You must prove you have a spouse, parent, or child who is a U.S. citizen or legal resident who would encounter **extreme hardship** without you.

WORK VISA: It is not possible to apply for a work visa if the visa you used to enter the United States has expired. If the visa you used to enter is still valid, you must apply for the work visa quickly with help from your prospective employer.

Read Chapter Three and learn what to do next. You may qualify for more than one of the above. The more, the better. A good Immigration Expert may submit multiple applications to improve your chances of success.

I Went to the Border and Officers Released Me into the United States

There is only one reason immigration officers would release you. That is, you claimed asylum. You went through a credible fear interview, and the officer found your story to be believable. The immigration officers released you into the United States with a future court date. If it has been less than a year since you entered, that is good news. Your best option is:

- ✓ **Asylum:** You have 12 months to fill out and file the Asylum Application (form **I-589**). You will have to report to Immigration Services regularly. **Be sure not to miss any appointments or court dates and inform the court when you move to a new address.** Asylum is one way to become documented, assuming you have a good story.

NOTE: If you are from **Mexico**, claiming asylum is more difficult, even with the violence there. This is because the United States Government still considers Mexico a democracy. To be granted asylum, you must have a believable story with proof that you will be harmed or killed if returned. Read *Chapter Four.*

What if you ignored the court hearings or did not complete the application? It is important that you contact an Immigration Expert as soon as possible. It is important to follow through with your asylum application unless you found a better option.

Warning

The MOST IMPORTANT PART for people coming into the United States and seeking asylum is passing the credible fear interview! If you were interviewed and are in the country, you passed. You must have a good asylum claim, and you will have to provide additional evidence within a year of entering the country. **Read** *Chapter Four,* **Developing Your Story.**

Important! your reason for being in the United States must be for fear of your life if you are returned to your home country. It cannot be for seeking a better life or to be with your family.

Other options for Becoming documented are:

✓ **Marriage Petition with the 601A Waiver:** You have a chance of receiving a green card if you **marry a U.S. citizen or legal resident**. Be aware that this approach is risky, as you will have to return to your home country, ask for a waiver, and prove that extreme hardship would occur to your spouse if you were to be separated. Know that this approach is risky.

✓ **Family Petition with the 601A Waiver:** If you have an immediate family member who is a U.S. citizen or legal resident, they can petition for you. You will have to go back to your home country, ask for a waiver, and prove that extreme hardship would occur to your petitioning family member. A U.S. citizen or legal resident who is over the age of 21 can petition for:
   o Parents
   o Spouse

Remember: The family or marriage petition is required to begin the process. Before you leave to your home country and ask for the waiver, you need the petition approved first.

- ✓ **Military Parole in Place:** If you entered without documentation but you have a spouse, child, or parent who is or was in the United States Military, the process is much simpler. You will **not** have to show hardship or go back to your home country. Once approved, you can apply for a green card in the U.S.

- ✓ **Battered Spouse (VAWA):** If you are married to a U.S. citizen or Green Card Holder who has physically or emotionally harmed you (domestic violence where the police were involved), you may qualify for a VAWA (Violence Against Women Act) petition.

- ✓ **Victim of a Crime in the United States (U-Visa):** This applies if you have been the victim of a crime while in the United States. For example, you were robbed, physically assaulted, raped, extorted, or beaten. If you reported the crime to the police, you might be eligible for a U-Visa. **See *Qualifying Crimes* at the end of this book for a full list of what crimes qualify.**

Remember

Read ***Chapter Three*** to learn what to do next. Remember, you may qualify for more than one option.

I Entered the United States without Being Caught; Authorities Do Not Know I Am Here

You came to the United States, but authorities (Immigration Services, **CBP**, **ICE**, police) have no record of you being here.

Your options for becoming documented are:

- ✓ **Asylum (Affirmative):** You may want to fill out an Asylum Application, **I-589**, if you have a fear of harm in your home country. It is important that you base your Asylum Application on **credible evidence proving that your home country is dangerous, you experienced serious trauma, and your life will be in danger if you are returned**. If it has been more than a year since you arrived, you must have a good reason why you did not file for asylum in the first year. You could use the reasons of trauma or sickness, for example.

- ✓ **Ten-Year Cancellation of Removal:** This is also known as the "42B." You must have lived in the United States for more than ten years without leaving the country. You will have to be in deportation court proceedings (for example, asylum) to apply. You must prove you have a spouse, parent, or child who is a U.S. citizen or legal resident who would encounter extreme hardship without you.

- ✓ **Victim of a Crime in the United States (U-Visa):** Even though you are undocumented, this applies if you have been the victim of a crime while here. For example, if you were robbed, physically assaulted, raped, extorted, or beaten, you might be eligible for a U-Visa. **See *Qualifying Crimes* at the end of this book for a full list of what qualifies.**

✓ **Marriage Petition or Family Petition with the 601A Waiver:** If you choose to become documented through marriage or family, at a certain point in this petition, **you MUST return to your home country. You must provide evidence that your U.S. citizen or legal resident spouse, child, or parent would suffer hardship if you were deported.**

Remember: The family or marriage petition is required to begin the process. Before you leave to your home country and ask for the waiver, you need the petition approved first.

✓ **BaBattered Spouse (VAWA, U-Visa):** This applies if you came into the country undocumented and married a U.S. citizen or Green Card Holder. If you are in an abusive relationship and you or your children are in danger because of your spouse, you may qualify for a VAWA or U-Visa.

✓ **Military Parole in Place:** If you came into the country undocumented but you have a spouse, child, or parent who is or was in the United States Military, the process is much simpler. If your petition is approved, you can initiate the green card process without having to leave the U.S.

Read *Chapter Three* and learn what to do next. You may qualify for more than one option.

I Was Never Caught Crossing the Border, but Now I Am in Deportation Court Proceedings

If you have lived in the United States for several years but were only recently caught by police or ICE, you must act quickly.

Your options for becoming documented are:

- ✓ **Asylum (Defensive):** You must have a credible story that if you are returned to your home country, your life would be in danger. You would need to fill out the form **I-589** and submit it along with evidence that your life would be in danger if you were to return to your home country.

- ✓ **Cancellation of Removal (42B):** If you have been here for ten years or more and you are in removal proceedings, you may qualify for a 42B. Also, you will have to submit evidence that your U.S. citizen spouse, parent, or child would experience extreme hardship if you were deported.

- ✓ **Marriage Petition with the 601A waiver:** You have a good chance of receiving a green card if you marry a United States citizen. However, you will have to return to your home country, ask for a waiver, and show that extreme hardship would be caused to your U.S. citizen or legal resident spouse if you were separated.

- ✓ **Family Petition with the 601A waiver:** If you have an immediate family member who is a U.S. citizen or legal resident, they can petition for you. You will have to go back to your home country and ask for a waiver. A U.S. citizen or legal resident petitioner who is over the age of 21 can petition for:

- o Spouse
- o Parents

Remember: The family or marriage petition is required to begin the process. Before you leave to your home country and ask for the waiver, you need the petition approved first.

✓ **Military Parole in Place:** If you came into the country undocumented but you have a spouse, child, or parent who is or was in the United States Military, the process is much simpler. You will **not** have to show hardship or go back to your home country and ask for a waiver. Once approved, you can obtain a green card through a family or marriage petition within the U.S.

✓ **Battered Spouse (VAWA, U-Visa, or Three-Year Cancellation of Removal):** If you are married to a U.S. citizen or Green Card Holder who has physically or emotionally harmed you (domestic violence act where the police were involved), you may be able to qualify for a VAWA petition.

✓ **Victim of a Crime in the United States (U-Visa):** Even though you are undocumented, this applies if you have been the victim of a crime while here. For example, if you were robbed, physically assaulted, raped, extorted, or beaten, and your crime was reported to the police, you might be eligible for a U-Visa. **See *Qualifying***

Crimes **at the end of this book for a full list of what qualifies.**

Read *Chapter Three* and learn what to do next. Remember, you may qualify for more than one option.

I Crossed the Border without Parents When I Was under the Age of 18: UAC

If you crossed the border when you were under the age of 18 without your parents, and you turned yourself in or got caught, your best option is:

✓ **UAC (Unaccompanied Alien Child) Asylum for Minors:** If you were under the age of 18 when you crossed the border without your parents, you were an **unaccompanied child.** No matter how old you are now, if you have documentation from the Office of Refugee Resettlement, you can still qualify for a UAC.

You most likely were given a court date and turned over to a legal guardian (relative or parent) or a shelter. It is important to find an Immigration Expert who can help you fill out the **I-589** for asylum for minors/UACs. It is also important to attend all court hearings. You must have a good argument as to why you came to the United States. If you tell Immigration Services that your parents sent you to the United States to make money or that you wanted to join your family here, you will be denied asylum. **Read *Chapter Four* to find out how to develop your story.**

Someone Brought Me to the United States against My Will or with a False Promise

Unfortunately, an underground network of people in the United States abuses unsuspecting immigrants. They bring people in with a visa under false promises, or they pay smugglers to bring people into the country for cheap labor or the sex industry. They bring people into the U.S. in one of two ways:

- ✓ They brought you in under a legal visa with the promise of work or some other purpose. Smugglers use several types of visas.
- ✓ They smuggled you into the country in a truck or shipping container, or through a border with no documentation.

How do you know if you are a victim of trafficking?
1. When you entered, someone took your passport away and forced you to perform work with little or no pay.
2. Your employer requires you to pay off a debt before you can be released.
3. They hold you against your will, and your employer does not allow you to come and go freely.
4. You are forced to provide sex for your employer or other people.
5. You are forced to work long hours, more than ten hours a day.
6. Your windows are covered with bars or wood. Cameras are watching your every move, and you are only allowed in public under threat of punishment if you disobey.

7. Your employer keeps the money you earn, with no explanation.

8. You are not allowed to speak to anyone outside of the business unless a boss is there.

9. They punish you or lock you up if you do not work or do not provide sex to their expectation.

If this is you, you must call the **National Human Trafficking Hotline for free at 1-888-373-7888.** Do not worry; these people will help you become safe and free. There is a good chance you will qualify for a T-Visa which will help you become documented and live freely in the United States. Your best option is:

✓ **Victim of Trafficking (T-Visa):** It is illegal for anyone to bring you to the United States either against your will or under false promises and force you to perform a job or sex under threat. The United States Government created the T-Visa to help victims of trafficking. **See** *Qualifying Crimes* **at the end of this book for a full list of what qualifies.**

If you have escaped from trafficking, but you are still living undocumented, there is nothing to stop ICE from catching and deporting you. If you report your experience of being forced into sex or labor as a trafficking crime, you could get a T-Visa and become documented. However, we highly suggest going to an Immigration Expert first and letting them help you report it. Chances are, the traffickers and abusers will be arrested, and the other victims could also qualify for visas.

STEP TWO:
If you are a DACA or TPS recipient, read the next chapter. Otherwise, go to *Chapter Three* and review your options based on how you arrived.

<u>Chapter Two</u>

TPS and DACA: How You Should Be Prepared

"We came to America, either ourselves or in the persons of our ancestors, to better the ideals of men, to make them see finer things than they had seen before, to get rid of the things that divide and to make sure of the things that unite." **–Woodrow Wilson**

What You Will Learn:

TPS: Temporary Protected Status
DACA: Deferred Action for Childhood Arrival

TPS: Temporary Protected Status

Introduction

On occasion, the president issues a temporary protected status to people whose lives may be at risk if returned to their home country due to a local natural disaster or war. You can receive temporary status as a current visa holder, a visa overstayer, or as an undocumented immigrant. If you comply with the rules established under the program, you can live and work in the United States without fear of deportation. However, it is temporary, and President Trump is attempting to end the program regardless of the continued problems in your home country.

I have Temporary Protected Status (TPS). Am I safe?
While many of these countries have been on the TPS list for years, it is extremely important to make alternative preparations and learn about other options *now* in case President Trump does end the program. You can obtain TPS only if you are from one of the approved countries and you are currently in the United States. **You can be a visa holder, be a visa overstayer, or be undocumented.** You can only sign up during each country's signup period. The president must renew or cancel the status of each country every 6-18 months. The countries still on the active list as of June 2018 are:

Country	Renew Date
Somalia	September 17, 2018
South Sudan	May 2, 2019
Syria	September 30, 2019
Yemen	March 3, 2020

The **"Renew Date"** means President Trump must decide on that date whether to extend the TPS program or terminate it. Though these countries are on the list because of ongoing disasters and wars, President Trump is removing as many countries from the TPS list as he can regardless of how dangerous conditions may still be. If the president terminates your country from the list, you will have about 18 months from that date to sell everything and return. President Trump has already canceled the TPS status program for the following countries:

Country	Must Return By
Haiti	July 22, 2019
Honduras	November 4, 2019
El Salvador	September 19, 2019
Nicaragua	January 5, 2019
Sudan	November 2, 2018
Nepal	June 24, 2019

"Must Return By" means you must return to your home country if you were under TPS and have not found another reason to stay by the date listed.

To obtain permanent status in the United States, you have the following options:

Remember

✓ **Marriage Petition:** Is there someone you are close to who is a citizen? Perhaps it is time to marry that person.

✓ **Family Petition:** Do you have a spouse, parent, or child (over the age of 21) who is a citizen or legal resident? They can petition for you to become documented.

NOTE: This applies only to TPS recipients who entered the U.S. without documentation. As a TPS recipient, depending on the state you live in (see list below) you have a unique opportunity to become legal through a Marriage Petition or Family Petition without having to go back to your home country for the **consular process**. This is only possible if you have obeyed the rules established in your TPS documentation and if you live in one of the states listed below:

California	Alaska
Arizona	Hawaii
Idaho	Montana
Nevada	Oregon
Washington	Kentucky
Michigan	Ohio
Tennessee	

NOTE: Even if you live in one of these states, if President Trump cancels the TPS program for your country and you have not adjusted your status, it is too late. You will have to consider other options.

For All Other States: The only way to avoid returning to your home country and having to ask for the waiver is to obtain an Application for Travel Document (**I-131** Advanced Parole). Once you have the travel document, you leave the country with it for a short period (even a few hours) and re-enter with this document. It gives you the legal entry you need to adjust your status in the United States. **This is only possible in combination with a Marriage Petition or Family Petition, and only if the Trump administration has not canceled the TPS program for your country.**

✓ **Military Parole in Place:** If you entered without inspection (a visa overstayer does not qualify), another option is to marry someone who is or was in the United States Military. Marrying someone in the military simplifies the process, and you do not have to leave the country for a waiver or show hardship. Once approved, you can apply for a green card through a marriage petition or family petition within the U.S.

For Marriage Petition or Family Petition: If you entered the United States on a visa, then you do not have to go back to your home country for a waiver regardless of which state you live in. In all scenarios, you will have to prove you have not committed any serious crimes and you have paid your taxes while working in accordance with your TPS document.

Other options to consider if Trump has canceled the TPS program for your country:

✓ **Asylum:** Even if Trump ends TPS for your country, it does not mean it is safe to go back. For example, El Salvador, like most Central American countries, is overrun with gangs, which may be even more dangerous than the natural disasters from years ago. Contact an Immigration Expert and ask them if you qualify for asylum. Remember, you will have to prove that being returned to your country will put your life in danger. Read *Chapter Four* on developing your story.

✓ **U-Visa:** If you have been a victim of a crime in the United States, you may qualify for a U-Visa. See *Qualifying Crimes* at the end of this book.

✓ **VAWA:** If you were or are in an abusive marriage with a U.S. citizen or legal resident, you may qualify.

✓ **Cancellation of Removal (42B):** If you have been in the United States for more than ten years and you have a spouse, parent, or child who is a U.S. citizen or legal permanent resident, you may qualify.

Read *Chapter Three* to learn more about which options might apply to you.

If you are a TPS recipient and want to stay in the United States, contact an Immigration Expert and discuss what you have read. **The Trump government has every intention of stopping the TPS program regardless of the conditions of your country, so do not wait.** Read *Chapter Seven* on how to find an Immigration Expert you can trust.

DACA: Deferred Action for Childhood Arrivals

Introduction

Though President Trump tried to cancel DACA in September 2017, two courts in the United States overruled the president and reinstated the program in early 2018. If you currently do not have DACA status, it is unlikely you will be able to apply. However, if you do, you can continue to extend it, and it is extremely important that you maintain your status or change it to a permanent status.

Unless the U.S. Congress votes to end the program, you will likely be safe for most of 2018 assuming you maintain your DACA status.

- ✓ Your DACA permit is valid until it expires, or you renew it. To determine when your permit expires, look at your **I-765** approval notice or your Employment Authorization Document (EAD) for your expiration date.
- ✓ Immigration Services will not accept or process any first-time applications.
- ✓ Advanced Parole (travel abroad) is no longer available. Immigration Services will not grant DACA recipients permission to travel abroad unless the courts decide otherwise. President Trump canceled the ability of DACA recipients to travel to other countries.

As a DACA recipient, you have the right to live and work in the United States without fear of **ICE** detaining and sending you to your birth country, provided you follow the rules as outlined in the documents with your approval notice. **You**

will lose your status and ICE will try to deport you if you commit any crimes or fail to follow any rules.

> **True Story:** Recently, a DACA recipient from Arizona was deported to Mexico because police found a gun and illegal drugs in a backpack that appeared to belong to him. Sadly, he could not handle the life in Mexico, and he killed himself. Take the DACA rules seriously. You will find useful information regarding DACA in the *Common Questions and Answers* section at the end of this book.

As a DACA recipient, you could become documented through a Marriage Petition (if you marry a U.S. citizen or legal resident) or Family Petition (if you have a spouse, child, or parent who is a U.S. citizen or legal resident). Details depend on the following situations:

✓ **You entered the United States with your parents on a visa, or you obtained Advanced Parole:** You can become documented without returning to your country of birth, asking for a waiver, or showing hardship for your petitioner.

✓ You entered the United States **with your parents but without documents**, and:
   o **You applied for and received DACA status before the age of 18:** If you received or even applied for DACA before the age of 18, you have not accrued any "**unlawful presence.**" Obtaining a green card through a Marriage Petition or Family Petition is fairly easy. You will have to go back to your birth country and attend a consular interview. The process is much easier than it was in the past and takes about a week.

- o **You applied for and received DACA status after the age of 18:** This is more difficult. You will have to go back to your home country, ask for a waiver, and prove hardship to your petitioner (The **I-601A** waiver process.) See *Chapter Three* Marriage or Family petition with **I-601A** waiver.
- o **You have a spouse, child, or parent who is or was in the United States Military:** This is a fairly easy process which is called **Parole in Place,** and you will not have to return to your country of birth for a waiver. Military Parole in Place is only available for people who entered without documentation. Once approved, you can apply for a green card through Marriage Petition or Family Petition in the U.S.

Remember, you start to accrue unlawful presence in the United States after you turn 18 years and six months old. This could have an impact on your application. Contact an Immigration Expert to understand your options.

Other options you may consider:

- ✓ **VAWA:** If your spouse is a legal resident or U.S. citizen and is abusing you (physically or emotionally), you can apply for VAWA without the abuser knowing. Abuse can be physical or mental.

- ✓ **U-Visa:** If you were the victim of a crime in the United States and someone reported it to the police, you could qualify.

- ✓ **Asylum:** This is a new idea, but a creative Immigration Expert could make a valid argument that if you are returned to your birth country, your life would be in danger because of being "Americanized." They could argue that you would be a target of gangs who may kidnap you, blackmail you, or force you into prostitution.

Go to *Chapter Three* and learn more about each of these options. Again, as we state so often in this book, seek legal advice from an Immigration Expert who can assist you with the process.

Chapter Three

Becoming Legal and Obtaining a Work Permit

"Everywhere immigrants have enriched and strengthened the fabric of American life." –John F. Kennedy

----

This chapter will teach you what options people in each of these categories have. Which categories best fit you?

- ✓ I am a visa overstayer and have married a U.S. citizen or Green Card Holder (Marriage Petition)
- ✓ I am a visa overstayer and have a close relative who is a U.S. citizen or Green Card Holder (Family Petition)
- ✓ I am undocumented (entered without inspection) and have married a U.S. citizen or Green Card Holder (Marriage Petition)
- ✓ I am undocumented (entered without inspection) and have a close relative who is a U.S. citizen or Green Card Holder (Family Petition)
- ✓ I am undocumented (entered without inspection) and have a spouse, child, or parent who is or was in the U.S. Military (Military Parole in Place)
- ✓ I entered the U.S. under the age of 18 with no parents or legal guardians, and I fear for my life if returned (UAC: Asylum for Unaccompanied Alien Child)
- ✓ If returned to my country, I fear being harmed or killed (Asylum)
- ✓ I have committed serious crimes, but if returned to my country I will be harmed, tortured, or killed **(CAT)**

✓ I have entered the U.S. more than once and have been caught, or I have committed minor crimes in the U.S., but would likely be harmed if returned (Withholding of Removal)

✓ I have been in the U.S. for ten years, and I have a U.S. citizen or legal resident spouse, child, or parent who is ill (42B Part 1)

✓ I have been in the U.S. for more than **three years**, and I am being emotionally or physically abused by my U.S. citizen or legal resident spouse, child, or parent (42B Part 2)

✓ My child or I am being emotionally or physically harmed by my U.S. citizen or legal resident spouse (VAWA)

✓ I am a victim of a crime on U.S. soil (U-Visa)

✓ I was brought to the U.S. and forced into the sex industry or forced labor (T-Visa)

✓ I am a witness to or know of serious crimes committed by gangs, the cartel, terrorists, or others in the U.S. (S-Visa)

✓ I am homeless in the U.S., under the age of 18, and have lost my parents or guardians (SIJS)

✓ I have no way to become documented at this time. What do I do?

ATTENTION: If you are a DACA or TPS recipient, go to *Chapter Two* and read about how you can become documented. Then refer to this chapter to better understand your options. See more DACA and TPS information in the *Common Questions and Answers* section at the end of this book.

Introduction

Many paths exist to obtain legal status. If you follow the rules, have a good argument along with convincing evidence, show up to the hearings, and have a little luck, you can make it.

In the first and second chapter we asked how you arrived and determined what your options are. This chapter will explain your options in more detail. Keep in mind, there may be more than one option you can apply for at the same time. So, read all of them and select the options that best fit you. Discuss them with your non-profit immigration office or Immigration Expert. It's possible they may file more than one application (for example: Asylum, 42B, and U-Visa).

In each category, you will learn whether your situation qualifies for a work permit, how to obtain it, and when you would be eligible. A work permit (EAD card) will enable you to legally work, receive a social security number, and obtain a U.S. driver license while waiting for a decision in your case.

Read this chapter carefully. Refer to *Chapter Four* and *Chapter Five* to properly build your case and, if necessary, represent yourself in court.

NOTE: You will find many duplicated sections as the filing processes are similar. Read the title, and if you think it might apply to you, read the entire section. Mark which ones might apply to you.

Remember, every case is different. Here we present ideas you can use when consulting with an Immigration Expert.

I Am a Visa Overstayer and Have Married a U.S. Citizen or Green Card Holder (Marriage Petition)

As a visa overstayer, if you marry a U.S. citizen or Green Card Holder, you can obtain a green card without going back to your home country for a waiver or showing hardship. You will have to prove your marriage is in good faith. It is technically illegal to use a Tourist Visa or most other visas to marry. However, if you convince Immigration Services that your marriage is real, they most likely will approve your application. Remember, overstaying your visa does subject you to the three-year or ten-year bar from re-entering the United States if you don't find a way to become documented.

If you are in a same-sex relationship: In 2015, the United States Supreme Court ruled in favor of same-sex marriage, which means that your application cannot be denied based on your sexual orientation.

Individual Requirements:
Proving your marriage was in good faith means producing documentation to support your application and demonstrating that you would be a good citizen of the United States. You can be in removal proceedings, but Immigration Services will review your application in greater detail. You will need to demonstrate that:

- ✓ You have not committed any serious crimes
- ✓ Your last entry into the United States was with a legal visa
- ✓ Your marriage was in good faith, with evidence to prove it

✓ Your spouse (sponsor) makes enough money to support you. If they do not, you will need a co-sponsor. The co-sponsor can be a U.S. citizen or legal permanent resident. Your combined household income must be:
  o Two people $25,032 (125% above poverty) per year
  o Three people $31,500 (125% above poverty) per year
  o Four people $37,969 (125% above poverty) per year

Even if you are working without permission, you can use your income to help qualify if you filed your taxes and have an ITIN: Individual Taxpayer Identification Number.

If your petitioner is a Green Card Holder, you are NOT immediately eligible to obtain a green card. Immigration Services limits the number of green cards issued to the beneficiary of a legal permanent resident. You must talk to an Immigration Expert to understand the process and waiting time. The process would be much easier if your petitioner became a citizen first.

The Process: A few weeks after your Immigration Expert has sent the Marriage Petition application (**I-130**) and supporting documents to Immigration Services, you will receive a receipt notice in the mail. This is the official document proving your papers are in process. **Make a copy of this notice and keep it with you in case you are pulled over or caught up in an ICE raid.**

A few weeks later you will receive a biometrics notice letter. The biometrics notice will tell you when and where to go to have your fingerprints taken.

The process can take several months to a year for the interview which both you and your spouse need to attend. If you pass your interview by proving your marriage is in good faith and you meet the individual requirements as listed above, then within a few weeks you will receive your green card.

Work Permit/EAD Card: When you file your green card petition based on marriage, you want to include the **I-765** work permit (EAD card) application. Most likely you will receive your EAD card within three or four months after filing. However, if your interview date is set for very soon (within a month or so), you may not need an EAD card for the waiting period.

NOTE: Pay attention to the expiration date on your EAD card. You want to apply for renewal three months before it expires. There would be an automatic extension of six months if you filed your renewal on time. That means you can work up to six months past the expiration date on your EAD card.

Filing Fees: Immigration Services fee $1760. Medical exam fee $200-400. Your Immigration Expert will charge additional fees for their services.

I Am a Visa Overstayer and Have a Close Relative Who Is a U.S. Citizen or Green Card Holder (Family Petition)

If you are a visa overstayer and have an immediate relative such as a spouse, parent, or child, you could qualify. However, many rules exist. As an overstayer, as long as your last entry was legal, you will not have to go back to your home country and ask for a waiver.

Individual Requirements: A successful Family Petition will include documentation that supports your application. You will need to demonstrate that:

- ✓ You have not committed any serious crimes
- ✓ Your last entry into the United States was with a legal visa
- ✓ Your petitioner makes enough money to support you. If they do not, you will need to have a co-sponsor. Your combined household income must be:
    - ○ Two people $25,032 (125% above poverty) per year
    - ○ Three people $31,500 (125% above poverty) per year
    - ○ Four people $37,969 (125% above poverty) per year

Even if you are working without permission, you can use your income to help qualify (as a household member) if you filed your taxes and have an ITIN: Individual Taxpayer Identification Number.

If your petitioner is a Green Card Holder, you are NOT immediately eligible to obtain a green card. Immigration Services limits the number of green cards issued to the beneficiary of a legal permanent resident. You must talk to an Immigration Expert to understand the process and waiting time. The process would be much easier if your petitioner became a citizen first.

The Process: A few weeks after your Immigration Expert has sent the Family Petition application (**I-130**) and supporting documents to Immigration Services, you will receive a receipt notice in the mail. This is the official document proving you have filed your papers with Immigration Services. **Make a copy of this notice and keep it with you in case you are pulled over or involved in an ICE raid.**

A few weeks later you will receive a biometrics notice. The biometrics notice will tell you when and where to go to have your fingerprints taken.

The process can take several months to a year for the interview which you need to attend. If you pass your interview, then within a few weeks you will receive your green card.

Work Permit/EAD Card: When you file your green card petition based on family, you want to include the **I-765** work permit application. Most likely you will receive your EAD card within three or four months after filing for your work permit. However, if your interview date is set for very soon (within a month or so), you may not need an EAD card for the waiting period.

NOTE: Pay attention to the expiration date on your EAD card. You want to apply for renewal three months before it expires.

There would be an automatic extension of six months if you filed your renewal on time. That means you can work up to six months past the expiration date on your EAD card.

Filing Fees: Immigration Services fee $1760. Medical exam fee $200-400. Your Immigration Expert will charge additional fees for their services.

I Am Undocumented and Have Married a U.S. Citizen or Green Card Holder (Marriage Petition)

People often think that marrying a U.S. citizen or legal resident is all it takes to become legal. However, there is more to the process.

If you entered without inspection: As an undocumented person who came across the border without a visa, obtaining a green card through marrying a U.S. citizen or legal resident is not so easy. Your Marriage Petition (**I-130**) will likely be approved, but then you must apply for a Provisional Unlawful Presence Waiver (**I-601A**) and prove that being separated from your spouse will cause them extreme hardship. Proving **extreme hardship** means providing proof such as medical or psychological records that your legal spouse would go through extreme mental or physical hardship if separated from you.

Once approved, you MUST go back to your home country for an interview at the United States Consulate. There are no guarantees. If the consular is convinced about your case, they will let you legally re-enter the United States, and you will be eligible for a green card. If not, Immigration Services could bar you from re-entering for three or ten years. It is entirely up to them. See *Chapter Four* on developing your hardship story.

If you are in a same-sex relationship: In 2015, the United States Supreme Court ruled in favor of same-sex marriage, which means that your application cannot be denied based on your sexual orientation.

ATTENTION: If you are under the age of 18 or it's been less than 180 days since you turned 18, you can go through the

consular process with a Marriage Petition (**I-130**). It is much easier than the Provisional Unlawful Presence Waiver (**I-601A**) and having to prove hardship. You will have to return to your country of birth before 180 days after your 18th birthday. The process is short.

Individual Requirements: Proving your marriage was in good faith means producing documentation to support your application such as photos, joint bank accounts, and joint leases or ownership of property. You will need to demonstrate that:

- ✓ You have not committed any serious crimes (in other words, you must be admissible)
- ✓ Your spouse would experience extreme hardship if separated from you
- ✓ Your spouse (sponsor) makes enough money to support you. Or, your combined household income must be:
  - o Two people $25,032 (125% above poverty) per year
  - o Three people $31,500 (125% above poverty) per year
  - o Four people $37,969 (125% above poverty) per year

Even if you are working without permission, you can use your income to help qualify (as a household member) if you filed your taxes and have an ITIN: Individual Taxpayer Identification Number.

If both of you do not meet the minimum income requirement, you can use a co-sponsor. However, due to recent application denials, its recommended that the co-sponsor be a family member.

The Process: If you entered without documentation, the process is more difficult than for visa holders or overstayers. Your Immigration Expert will file the Marriage Petition application (**I-130**). After it is approved, your Immigration Expert will initiate the immigration process and submit the Provisional Unlawful Presence Waiver (**I-601A**). Once this waiver is approved, you will receive your interview date at a consulate in your home country. If all goes well at the interview, you will receive a green card.

> **Remember:** The family or marriage petition is required to begin the process. Before you leave to your home country and ask for the waiver, you need the petition approved first.

Work Permit/EAD Card: No work permit is available during the application process.

Filing Fees: Provisional Unlawful Presence Waiver (**I-601A**) $630. Marriage Petition (**I-130**) $535. Consular Process $325 + $120. Biometrics $85. Your Immigration Expert will charge additional fees for their services.

I Am Undocumented and Have a Close Family Member Who Is a U.S. Citizen or Green Card Holder (Family Petition)

If you entered the United States without inspection (no documentation), only certain close family members can petition for you under the Family Petition (**I-130**). Once this petition is approved, your Immigration Expert will initiate the **I-601A** waiver process. You will have to prove that being separated from your petitioning family (parent or spouse only) member will cause extreme hardship to them. It's also good if you can prove that you have been providing most of the income for the family, and that your petitioning family member cannot work or can only work part-time. Once approved, you MUST go back to your home country for an interview at the United States Consulate. See *Chapter Four* on developing your hardship story.

NOTE: The qualifying relative for the I601-A waiver does not have to be the petitioning family member on the I-130 application (which is needed only to initiate the I-601A waiver process). The extreme hardship for the waiver, is separate from the **I-130** Family Petition (can be two different people). You may also have more than one qualifying family member for the petition (for example, father and spouse).

Individual Requirements: A successful Family Petition will include documentation that supports your application. You will need to demonstrate that:

- ✓ You have not committed any serious crimes
- ✓ Your petitioning family member would experience extreme hardship if separated from you

✓ You and your family make enough money to support you. If not, you may have a co-sponsor. Your combined household income must be:
- o Two people $25,032 (125% above poverty) per year
- o Three people $31,500 (125% above poverty) per year
- o Four people $37,969 (125% above poverty) per year

If you live together, you can use your income to help qualify, even if you are working without permission.

If the petitioning family members do not meet the minimum income requirement, you can use a co-sponsor. However, due to recent application denials, its recommended that the co-sponsor be a family member.

ATTENTION: If you are under the age of 18 or it's been less than 180 days since you turned 18, you can go through the consular process with a Marriage Petition (**I-130**). It is much easier than the Provisional Unlawful Presence Waiver (**I-601A**) and having to prove hardship. You will have to return to your country of birth before 180 days after your 18th birthday. The process is short.

The Process: If you entered without documentation, the process is more difficult than for visa holders or overstayers. Your Immigration Expert will file the Family Petition (**I-130**). After it is approved, your Immigration Expert will initiate the immigration process and submit the Provisional Unlawful Presence Waiver (**I-601A**). Once this waiver is approved, you will receive your interview date at a U.S. Consulate in your home country. If all goes well during the interview, you will receive a green card.

Again, you must prove that your petitioner (your family member who is a U.S. citizen or legal resident) would suffer extreme hardship without you (for example, you could provide medical or psychological records). Read the Extreme Hardship section in *Chapter Four*.

Remember: The family or marriage petition is required to begin the process. Before you leave to your home country and ask for the waiver, you need the petition approved first.

Work Permit/EAD Card: No EAD work permit card is available during the application process.

Filing Fees: Provisional Unlawful Presence Waiver (**I-601A**) $630. Family Petition (**I-130**) $535. Consular Process $325 + $120. Biometrics $85. Your Immigration Expert will charge additional fees for their services.

I Am Undocumented and Have a Spouse, Parent, or Child Who Is or Was in the U.S. (Military Parole in Place)

NOTE: This also applies to parents or unmarried children (under the age of 21) of military members. If you have a son, daughter, father, or mother who is or was in the U.S. Military, you could qualify for a green card through the same petition. Instead of providing a marriage certificate, you provide a birth certificate.

The path to a green card with this petition is easier, as the United States loves their military people. Parole in Place is only for people who entered the United States without inspection (undocumented). If Immigration Services approves the petition, your undocumented entry will be forgiven. However, Military Parole in Place is "discretionary." That means it is up to each local immigration field office. Military Parole in Place is only eligible to relatives of active or honorably discharged military members.

Individual Requirements:
- ✓ You must have entered the United States without inspection
- ✓ You must not have committed any serious crimes
- ✓ Your petitioner (spouse, child, or parent) must be in the U.S. Military or be a veteran

The Process: Complete the **I-131** form and include:
- ✓ Proof of military service (current or honorably discharged)
- ✓ Proof of marriage or family relationship
- ✓ Affidavits (written statements) about your good

standing in your community written by friends, family, neighbors, or employers
✓ Copy of your current passport or ID

Send the documents to your local immigration field office and wait for the appointment. The interview is short. Once you are approved, you are eligible to file for your green card without having to leave the country. With your documents, you will now apply for permanent residence or adjust status based on marriage. Once you go through the entire process, you will receive your green card.

Work Permit/EAD Card: When you file your green card petition based on marriage, you want to include the **I-765** work permit application. Most likely you will receive your EAD card within three or four months after filing for your work permit. However, if your interview date is set for very soon (within a month or so), you may not need an EAD card for the waiting period.

NOTE: Pay attention to the expiration date on your EAD card. You want to apply for renewal three months before it expires. There would be an automatic extension of six months if you filed your renewal on time. That means you can work up to six months past the expiration date on your EAD card.

Filing Fees: There is no filing fee for Military Parole in Place. Application fee for green card based on marriage $1760. Medical exam $200-400. Your Immigration Expert will charge additional fees for their services.

I Entered the U.S. under the Age of 18 Unaccompanied by Parents or Legal Guardians, and Fear for My Life If Returned (UAC: Asylum for Unaccompanied Child)

UAC (Unaccompanied Alien Child) refers to a person under the age of 18 who crossed the border without parents or legal guardians and is seeking asylum in the United States because they were threatened, harassed, persecuted, or mistreated in their home country.

It is important to say that your reason for coming to the United States was out of fear—NOT because you were seeking a better life or because you wanted to be with your parents.

Different Situations of UAC:
- ✓ You crossed the border without parents or legal guardians and you were caught, or you handed yourself over to Immigration Services.
    - o In this case, Immigration Services issued you documents recognizing you as a UAC. These documents are important when you file your Asylum Application.
- ✓ You crossed the border, you are still under the age of 18, and Immigration Services does not know you are here.
    - o In this case, you MUST file your UAC application BEFORE you turn 18, even if you are living with your parents or legal guardian. Your UAC application approval depends on your asylum story. See *Chapter Four* on developing your story.
- ✓ You are in removal proceedings, are under the age of 18, and have no lawful status.

o In this case, you should file your Asylum Application BEFORE you turn 18. Obtaining legal status all depends on your asylum story.

If you entered the United States under the age of 18 but are **now over 18** and Immigration Services does not know you are here, it is too late for UAC Asylum. You will have to apply for Affirmative Asylum.

It would be wise to find an Immigration Expert or a non-profit organization that will help you with an Application for Asylum (Form **I-589**). You have one year from the time you arrived to apply. If it has been more than one year, a good Immigration Expert along with a good reason (such as that you didn't understand the system, or you were simply too fearful for your life) can overcome this problem.

Individual Requirements:
- ✓ You were under the age of 18 when you entered the U.S.
- ✓ You have written proof from the **Office of Refugee Resettlement** that you entered as a UAC
- ✓ You have a fear for your life story if returned to your home country
- ✓ You have not committed any serious crimes

The Process: When you enter the United States as a minor (under the age of 18) and have a good reason why you want to apply for asylum, you have a good chance of being allowed to stay in the United States. If you had no parents or family in the United States, Immigration Services would have provided you a place to stay. Remember, testimony alone (a story without proof) is often enough for Immigration Services if they believe your story. Read *Chapter Four* on how to develop your story.

You will need to file the Application for Asylum (**I-589**). The process is much easier than if you were an adult. You will have to attend an interview with an asylum officer. The interview process for UAC Asylum is friendlier and easier to pass than Affirmative or Defensive Asylum. **Remember, it ALL depends on your story.** An Immigration Expert or a non-profit immigration organization will help you with the process.

Work Permit/EAD Card: After submitting your application to Immigration Services, you will receive a receipt notice. There will be a date stamped on the notice. From this date forward, you count 150 days. After that, you can submit your work permit application. You will receive your work permit about three months later. The card is good for up to two years while you are in proceedings. You can continue to renew it until the process is complete. There is no filing fee for the first application, but each renewal will require a filing fee of $410.

NOTE: Pay attention to the expiration date on your EAD card. You want to apply for renewal three months before it expires. There would be an automatic extension of six months if you filed your renewal on time. That means you can work up to six months past the expiration date on your EAD card.

> **ATTENTION:** If you are planning on moving to a new state while you are in proceedings, doing so will "stop the 180-day clock." Stopping the clock extends the period it takes for you to obtain your EAD card. Once you have the EAD card, you can use it in any state to get a job. We suggest that you do not move or make any changes to your application during the first 180 days.

Filing Fees: There is no filing fee for the UAC Asylum Application. Your Immigration Expert will charge fees for their services.

If Returned to My Country, I Fear Being Harmed or Killed (Asylum)

As an undocumented person in the United States, understand that asylum could be your only chance to become legal. Claiming asylum will allow you to stay in the United States indefinitely if you have a credible fear of being returned to your home country. No specific list of countries exists that would automatically approve your application. If you come from an industrialized country such as Germany, Canada, or Australia for example, this option is NOT for you. **NOTE: For any asylum case, testimony alone is often enough proof. However, it is very helpful to have evidence to help prove your story.** You have one year from the time you arrived in the U.S. to apply for asylum. If you have already missed that deadline, a good Immigration Expert along with a good reason (such as that you didn't understand the system, or you were simply too fearful for your life) can overcome this problem.

Here are some questions that will help you know if you qualify for asylum:
- ✓ Did you come to the United States because you fear either physical or psychological harm in your home country?
- ✓ Did you come to the United States because you experienced a personal trauma in your home country?
- ✓ Did you come to the United States because your family was threatened, harmed, or killed in your home country?
- ✓ Are you part of a religious group that is discriminated against and often tortured or killed in your home country?

✓ Does your profession (politician, social organizer, teacher, or other position that the government sees as a threat) in your home country put your life at risk of harm?

✓ Are gangs out of control in your home country? Do you have evidence or a story of them trying to recruit you or your children? And are the police corrupt or do they refuse to help?

✓ Have you reported or in some way cooperated with law officials in your home country about crimes or gang activities, and been threatened because of your knowledge?

✓ Is your race or caste discriminated against to the degree that your life would be in danger if returned to your home country?

✓ Were you sexually or physically abused in your home country? And would the abuse continue, or would society reject you based on local customs if returned to your home country?

✓ Were you a victim of forced sex or slave labor in your home country? And would this happen to you again if returned?

✓ Would you or your children be severely discriminated against in your home country because you are a woman or are gay?

✓ Are you certain that regardless of where you lived in your country, you would be in fear for your life?

If any of the above fits you, asylum is a good option. You must explain that you fear if you are deported back, you would experience trauma, severe harassment, threats, or death. A good Immigration Expert will help you build your case.

It is very helpful to have supporting evidence such as newspaper articles, physical scars, psychological reports from a U.S. psychologist, and possibly police reports explaining your story. Even if you have lived in the United States for 20 years, you can apply for asylum. **However, before you do anything, read about developing your asylum story in** *Chapter Four*.

Individual Requirements:
  ✓ Most importantly, you need to have a good fear story
  ✓ It's best if you applied for asylum within one year of your arrival
  ✓ If it has been more than one year, you will need a good story as to why you did not apply
  ✓ You must have not committed any serious crimes
  ✓ You must be over the age of 18 (If under age 18, see UAC in this chapter)

There are two types of asylum, Affirmative and Defensive. Affirmative Asylum is if you are not in removal proceedings (Immigration Services does not know you are here) or you entered with a visa. Defensive Asylum is if you are in removal court proceedings. The law states you must apply for asylum within the first year you entered the United States. However, again, a good fear story and knowledgeable Immigration Expert can get you around this rule.

The process for the two types of asylum is different:
  ✓ **Affirmative Asylum:** An asylum officer interviews you (no ICE lawyer is present), and you must bring your interpreter if you don't speak English.
  ✓ **Defensive Asylum:** You will appear in a court hearing in front of a judge, and an ICE lawyer is present to cross-examine and try to disqualify your story. The court will provide an interpreter.

Your asylum-claim story and your reason for why you came to the United States is the same for either Affirmative Asylum or Defensive Asylum.

Affirmative Asylum

You are not in removal proceedings and were never arrested (no one knows you are here). Or you entered on a visa, and your visa is still valid, or you overstayed your visa. You will have to submit your Asylum Application to Immigration Services (**USCIS**). Remember you will have to have an asylum story. **You should apply within the first year of arrival. If you have been here longer than a year, you may still qualify, but do not try this alone. Work with a non-profit immigration office or Immigration Expert.**

It could be a few months to a year before you receive your asylum interview date. You want to use this time to prepare your story. Read *Chapter Four* on developing your story. After the interview, you will be either denied or approved. If approved, you will become an Asylee. After one year, you can then apply for a green card.

If the immigration officer denies your application, they will refer you to a judge and put you into removal proceedings. You will then have a second chance to tell your story in court. **Remember, in court you will also be up against the ICE lawyer.** If the judge believes your story and gives you Asylee status, after one year you can then apply for a green card. If the judge also denies you, you have two options:

1) You sign a voluntary departure. You will have 60-120 days to prepare your departure and leave the country voluntarily. It is a good option because you will not have a three-year or ten-year bar on your immigration record. You can apply for a visa in the future. Be aware of certain rules to qualify for the voluntary departure.

2) You can appeal the judge's decision. The next appeal will cost more money because you cannot do this

without a lawyer, but it can buy you more time in the United States. The process of the three appeals takes approximately three to five years. If you lose the final appeal, you must return to your home country, and you will face the three-year or ten-year bar against re-entry.

Work Permit/EAD Card: After you have submitted your Asylum Application (**I-589**), you will receive a receipt notice with a date. Then count 150 days forward. On that date, you can apply for your work permit. In about three months, you will receive your EAD card. You will not have to pay filing fees with the first application. For every renewal, you will have to pay a $410 filing fee. Along with your work permit (EAD card), you will receive your Social Security number. With that, you can obtain a state driver license.

NOTE: Pay attention to the expiration date on your EAD card. You want to apply for renewal three months before it expires. There would be an automatic extension of six months if you filed your renewal on time. That means you can work up to six months past the expiration date on your EAD card.

ATTENTION: If you are planning on moving to a new state while you are in proceedings, doing so will "stop the 180-day clock." Stopping the clock extends the period it takes for you to obtain your EAD card. Once you have the card, you can use it in any state to get a job. **We suggest that you do not move or make any changes to your application during the first 180 days.**

Defensive Asylum

This means you have been caught or detained either at the border or within the country. You will have to defend yourself in court.

You will complete the Asylum Application (**I-589**), file it with the court, and send a copy to the Immigration and **Customs Enforcement (ICE) Office**. You must inform the court that you are applying for asylum at your initial hearing (master hearing). Read *Chapter Five* on defending yourself in court. **We urge you not to try this without an Immigration Expert.**

At your master hearing, you will appear and receive a notice for your next master hearing or individual hearing. Once you have your date for your individual hearing, you should begin to prepare your case by gathering evidence. For example, you could find newspaper articles about problems in your home country, collect letters from friends and family, write your personal statement, or get a report from a psychologist supporting your story. Refer to *Chapter Four* for details on how to develop your story.

The process of organizing documents and knowing where and when to send them is complicated. We suggest you either contact a non-profit immigration service for help or hire an Immigration Expert to assist you. Read *Chapter Four* on **developing your story** and if necessary, *Chapter Five* on **representing yourself in court.**

Remember, in court you will also be up against the ICE lawyer whose job is to convince the judge to deny your application and deport you. The better you are prepared, the better your chances of success.

At the individual court hearing, you will have the opportunity to tell your story to the judge. If the judge believes your story and approves your case, you receive Asylee status, and after one year, you can petition for a green card. If the judge denies you, you have two options:

1) You can sign a **voluntary departure**. You will have 60-120 days to prepare your departure and leave the country voluntarily. It is a good option because you will not have any three-year or ten-year bars on your immigration record. You can apply for a visa in the future. Know that voluntary departure has certain requirements.

2) You can appeal the judge's decision. The next appeal will cost more money because you cannot do this without a lawyer, but it can buy you more time in the United States. The appeal process takes approximately three to five years. You can appeal up to three times. If you lose the final appeal, you must return to your home country, and you will face the three-year or ten-year bar against re-entry.

Work Permit/EAD Card: The court will stamp your original Asylum Application with the receipt date. From that date on, count 150 days. On that date, you can apply for a work permit. You will receive your EAD card about three months after that. With the work permit, you will receive your Social Security number. That will allow you to apply for a state driver license. You will not have to pay filing fees with the first application. For every renewal, you will have to pay a $410 filing fee.

Filing Fees: There is no filing fee for the Application for Asylum (**I-589**). Your Immigration Expert will charge fees for their services.

I Have Committed Serious Crimes, but If Returned to My Country I Will Be Harmed, Tortured, or Killed (CAT)

Convention Against Torture (CAT): CAT is limited to people who have committed serious crimes in the United States and have a greater than 50% certainty that if returned to their home country, they would be severely harmed or killed. Obtaining CAT protection is difficult.

Like Withholding of Removal, the protection under CAT is mandatory if you meet all the requirements.

You must demonstrate that you would experience intentional and severe physical or mental pain by your home country government, or that your home country government would allow others to cause you intentional and severe pain.

If you are ineligible for asylum and Withholding of Removal, and you have committed aggravated felonies, Convention Against Torture (CAT) is your only chance to remain in the United States.

Aggravated felony requirement:
- ✓ Have you been sentenced to a combined total of five or more years in prison for convictions of aggravated felonies?
- ✓ Did you have criminal convictions related to selling or smuggling drugs?
- ✓ Have you been involved in significant violence, harm, or a serious risk to others?
- ✓ Have you supported or participated in terrorist groups?

Keep in mind, CAT is the lowest level of asylum and the most difficult to obtain. It means you will never be eligible for a green card or citizenship.

If you obtain CAT:
- ✓ You will be required to pay an annual fee for your work permit.
- ✓ You can never travel outside of the United States.
- ✓ The U.S. Government has the right to move you to another country other than your home country.
- ✓ You may be deported back to your home country if conditions change there.

Sometimes you will end up with an "order of supervision." It means you will have to check in with Immigration Services on a regular basis and you will have to request permission before you move to another state.

Individual Requirements:
- ✓ You must be able to prove that you will most likely be harmed or killed if returned to your home country.
- ✓ Your home country government must be involved in or at least consent to your harm.
- ✓ You must have committed serious crimes in the United States that make you ineligible for asylum or Cancellation of Removal.

The Process: CAT applicants must complete an Asylum Application (**I-589**). Even with extensive evidence and witnesses, CAT applications are often denied because of the high standards applicants must meet. It is essential that you work with an Immigration Expert on your case.

Work Permit/EAD Card: If you are not in detention or prison when you apply, the court will stamp your original

Asylum/Withholding of Removal Application with a receipt date. From that date on, count 150 days. On that date, you can apply for a work permit. You will receive your EAD card about three months after that. With the work permit, you will receive your Social Security number. That will allow you to apply for a state driver license. There is no filing fee for the first work permit application. You will have a $410 filing fee for future applications after that.

Filing Fees: There is no filing fee for the CAT Application/Asylum Application (**I-589**). Your Immigration Expert will charge fees for their services.

I Have Entered the U.S. More Than Once and Have Been Caught, or I Have Committed Minor Crimes in the U.S., and Would Be Harmed if Returned (Withholding of Removal)

Withholding of Removal is a special order decided by an immigration judge. You must prove a higher than 50% chance of harm if returned to your home country.

Withholding of Removal is for people who would not qualify for asylum because they have committed certain types of crimes such as multiple re-entries or too many DUIs, for example. Consult with an Immigration Expert for a complete list. There is no deadline to file, and it is NOT discretionary. That means, if you prove you are eligible for withholding, a judge MUST grant your application.

Keep in mind, Withholding of Removal is a lower level of asylum. **That means you will never be able to apply for a green card or citizenship.**
If you obtain Withholding of Removal:
- ✓ You will be required to pay an annual fee for your work permit.
- ✓ You can never leave the United States.
- ✓ The U.S. Government has the right to move you to another country other than your home country.

Sometimes you will end up with an "order of supervision." It means you will have to check in with Immigration Services on a regular basis and you will have to request permission before you move to another state.

A big difference between asylum and Withholding of Removal is that the evidence for Withholding of Removal must be stronger and unquestionable (country reports, personal witnesses, physical scars). You must prove that you would be harmed if returned to your home country.

Individual Requirements:
- ✓ You must be able to prove that you will be harmed or killed if returned to your home country.
- ✓ You must have committed minor crimes in the United States that make you ineligible for asylum.

The Process: The application is the same form as an Application for Asylum (**I-589**). Only a judge can grant Withholding of Removal. **Refer to the asylum section in this chapter and read *Chapter Four* on developing your story.** If you lose, you have two options:

1) You can appeal the judge's decision. This process will cost more money, and you cannot do this without a lawyer. The appeal can buy you more time, approximately three to five years during which you can work. You can appeal up to three times. If you lose the final appeal, you must return to your home country, and you will face the three or ten-year bar on re-entering the U.S.
2) **Voluntary Departure**: You can allow Immigration Services to deport you.

Work Permit/EAD Card: The court will stamp your original Asylum/Withholding of Removal Application with a receipt date. From that date on, count 150 days. On that date, you can apply for a work permit. You will receive your EAD card about three months after that. With the work permit, you will receive your Social Security number. That will allow you to apply for a state driver license. You will have to pay for a new EAD card every year while your case is pending.

Filing Fees: There is no filing fee for the Asylum/Withholding of Removal Application (**I-589**). Your Immigration Expert will charge fees for their services.

> **ATTENTION**: If you are planning on moving to a new state while you are in proceedings, doing so will "stop the 180-day clock." Stopping the clock extends the period it takes for you to obtain your EAD card. Once you have the card, you can use it in any state to get a job. We suggest that you do not move or make any changes to your application during the first 180 days.

I Have Been in the U.S. for Three to Ten Years (42B Cancellation of Removal)

Ten-Year Cancellation of Removal: 42B Part 1

The **Ten-Year Cancellation of Removal** only happens if you are already in proceedings. You will have received a **Notice to Appear (NTA)** letter from ICE (a paper giving you reasons why ICE thinks they should deport you). A 42B is difficult to obtain, and you must be prepared to provide a credible argument as to why the court should cancel your deportation order. If the court agrees with your reason, you could change your status and receive a green card.

Individual Requirements: You will be allowed to eventually receive a green card if you meet ALL the following requirements:

✓ You can prove you have lived in the U.S. for more than ten years before the date of your Notice to Appear, and you have not left the U.S. for more than a three-month period. Examples of proof include bank statements, lease agreements, and school records of children.

✓ You have a parent, spouse, or child who is a U.S. citizen or permanent resident, and most importantly, you can prove that this person is mentally or physically ill and that your deportation would cause extreme hardship to them. A good Immigration Expert can help you with this process. Read *Chapter Four* on developing your hardship story

✓ You have been a good person in your community and can demonstrate "good moral character." You will have to prove this with letters from friends and employers.

✓ You have had no serious criminal convictions.

✓ You are in removal court proceedings.

The Ten-Year Clock: You will have to prove you have continuously lived in the United States for at least ten years. The clock starts the moment you can prove you were in the United States. This can be proven with receipts, check stubs, U.S. birth certificates of your children, written letters from people who know you, and more. The clock stops the when you either leave the United States for more than 90 days or you receive a Notice to Appear. If you cannot convince the court you have lived here for at least ten years, you will not qualify for Cancellation of Removal.

The Process: You and your Immigration Expert will fill out and submit the 42B application. Usually, this will happen before your master hearing. There may be more than one master hearing. At this point, you do not have to provide evidence. Soon after your master hearing(s), you should start to collect evidence to support your case for your individual hearing. You will need to collect many documents. Examples include medical and psychological records of your legal spouse or children that show how they would experience hardship if separated from you, affidavits from friends that show you have established roots in the community, pay stubs, lease agreements, tax documents, and more. These are necessary to prove how long you have been in the United States and to show the connection to your family and community. See *Chapter Four* on building your story.

Next is your individual hearing. If the judge rules against you, you have a chance to appeal their decision (you can apply for up to three appeals). We explain the court process in *Chapter Five*. The appeal process can take three to five years.

Work Permit/EAD Card: The court will stamp your original 42B application with the receipt date. From that date on, count 150 days. On this date, you can apply for a work permit. You will receive your EAD card about three months after your work permit application. With the work permit, you will receive your Social Security number. That will allow you to apply for a state driver license. You will have to pay an application fee of $410. For every renewal (once a year), you will have to pay $410.

NOTE: Pay attention to the expiration date on your EAD card. You want to apply for renewal three months before it expires. There would be an automatic extension of six months if you filed your renewal on time. That means you can work up to six months past the expiration date on your EAD card.

Filing Fees: Executive Office for Immigration Review (EOIR-42B) $100. Biometrics $85. EAD card/work permit $410. Your Immigration Expert will charge additional fees for their services.

Three-Year Cancellation of Removal: 42B Part 2

The **Three-Year Cancellation of Removal** only happens if you are already in proceedings. You will have received a **Notice to Appear (NTA)** letter from ICE (a paper giving you reasons why ICE thinks they should deport you). You must be prepared to provide a credible argument as to why the court should cancel your deportation order. If the court agrees with your reason, you could change your status and receive a green card.

Individual Requirements: You will have to meet ALL the following requirements:

- ✓ You have been in the United States for more than three years and have been subject to extreme cruelty by your U.S. citizen or permanent resident spouse or parent. OR, you have a child (under the age of 18) who is being mistreated by your U.S. citizen or permanent resident spouse.
- ✓ Your removal would result in extreme hardship to you or your U.S. citizen/legal permanent resident child. OR, your child is in removal proceedings, and his or her deportation would result in extreme hardship to the child or you.
- ✓ You have been a good person in your community and can demonstrate "good moral character." You will have to prove this with letters from friends and employers.
- ✓ You have no serious criminal convictions. such as DUI or domestic violence charges.
- ✓ You must be in removal court proceedings.

The Process: You and your Immigration Expert will fill out and submit the 42B application. Usually, it is before your master hearing. There may be more than one master hearing. At this point, you do not have to provide evidence. Soon after your master hearing(s), you should start to collect evidence to support your case for your individual hearing. You will need to collect many documents. Examples include police reports documenting the abuse, medical records of injuries, psychological records of you or your child (depression, anxiety, or trauma due to the mistreatment). **You will also need to provide proof that you have been in the United States for more than three years.**

Next is your individual hearing. If the judge rules against you, you have a chance to appeal his or her decision (you can apply for up to three appeals). We explain the court process in *Chapter Five*. The appeal process can take two to three years.

Work Permit/EAD Card: The court will stamp your original 42B application with the receipt date. From that date on, count 150 days. On that date, you can apply for a work permit. You will receive your EAD card about three months after your work permit application. With the work permit, you will receive your Social Security number. That will allow you to apply for a state driver license. You will have to pay filing fees of $410. For every renewal (once a year), you will have to pay $410.

NOTE: Pay attention to the expiration date on your EAD card. You want to apply for renewal three months before it expires. There would be an automatic extension of six months if you filed your renewal on time. That means you can work up to six months past the expiration date on your EAD card.

Filing Fees: Executive Office for Immigration Review (EOIR-42B) $100. Biometrics $85. EAD card/work permit $410. Your Immigration Expert will charge additional fees for their services.

My Child or I Am Being Emotionally or Physically Harmed by My U.S. Citizen or Legal Resident Spouse, Parent, or Adult Child (VAWA)

The VAWA (Violence Against Women Act) is designed to protect **women AND men** in the United States who are victims of crimes committed against them by their U.S. citizen or legal resident spouse, parent, or adult child (over age 18). If you are undocumented or a visa overstayer living in the United States and your legal resident spouse—man or woman—physically, emotionally, or sexually abuses either you, your children, or your spouse's children, you can get out of the relationship and obtain a green card. Once approved, you are immediately eligible for permanent residency (green card). **You can "self-petition" which means you go through the process without your spouse or anyone in your family knowing**.

Individual Requirements:
- ✓ You must be currently living with your spouse, parent, or adult child who is causing emotional or physical violence to you or to your children who are unmarried and under the age of 21, OR:
- ✓ If you have moved out and/or gotten divorced, and you are living in the United States with no documentation, it must be less than two years since the separation or divorce.
- ✓ You must have good moral character.
- ✓ You must have proof of marriage to or family relationship to the U.S. citizen or permanent resident who is abusing you or your children.
- ✓ You must have proof of the abuse they caused while you were together, such as police records, hospital receipts, or witness testimony.

If your fiancé brought you to the United States on a visa but did not marry you, you would not qualify. You would have to seek the advice of a non-profit legal aid or Immigration Expert to find another way out such as a U-Visa or asylum.

The Process: The best way to get help is to call the **National Domestic Violence Hotline**: 1-800-799-7233. It is free to call. The hotline is completely confidential, the workers speak English and Spanish, and they can help you with the VAWA process by connecting you with someone who lives close to you. The hotline workers will not inform any family member or authorities such as ICE, and they will not deport you. You can also contact any Immigration Expert or non-profit immigration office. See *Chapter Seven*.

- ✓ **If your abusive spouse, child, or parent is a U.S. citizen:** You can apply for your green card at the same time as your VAWA application (form **I-360**).
- ✓ **If your abusive spouse, child, or parent is a Green Card Holder:** You will have to wait for approval of your VAWA petition first before applying for a green card yourself. It can take up to one year to receive approval.

IF YOU ARE IN THE ACT OF BEING ABUSED AND YOU FEAR FOR YOUR LIFE OR THE LIFE OF YOUR CHILDREN, DIAL 911.

Work Permit/EAD Card:
- ✓ **If your abuser is a U.S. citizen:** You will attach your work permit application (**I-765**) to your VAWA application (**I-360**). While waiting for approval, you will receive your EAD card within three or four

months.

✓ **If your abuser is a Green Card Holder**: You will still attach your work permit application (**I-765**) to your VAWA application (**I-360**), but you will have to wait until your VAWA petition is approved to receive your EAD card. It can take up to one year before you receive your approval.

NOTE: Pay attention to the expiration date on your EAD card. You want to apply for renewal three months before it expires. There would be an automatic extension of six months if you filed your renewal on time. That means you can work up to six months past the expiration date on your EAD card.

Filing Fees: There is no filing fee for the VAWA application. Green card petition $1140. Biometrics $85. Fee waivers are available if you have a low income. Your Immigration Expert will charge additional fees for their services.

I Am a Victim of a Crime on U.S. Soil (U-Visa)

The U-Visa (Application for U Nonimmigrant Status, form **I-918**) is for victims of crime who are willing to help law enforcement. Have you ever been a victim of a crime in the United States? For example, have you been robbed, raped, beaten, held hostage, blackmailed, or forced into labor with little or no pay? Have you been a victim of any crime where the police were involved? Or, did you witness a crime that caused you severe mental problems, such as being unable to sleep or afraid to leave your house? This too can qualify if you have police reports of the crime and records from a psychologist proving your condition.

To Qualify for a U-Visa:
 ✓ The crime must have occurred in the United States
 ✓ You must have suffered physical or mental abuse
 ✓ You must have reported the crime to the police, so a record exists
 ✓ You must be of help to the police and or prosecutor in the investigation

Being the victim of or witness to a crime can be used to obtain a green card if you work with the police to solve the crime. Even if the crime does not get solved, what matters is your willingness to help the police. Review the list of specific crimes that qualify in the *Qualifying Crimes* section at the end of this book.

Individual Requirements:
 ✓ A copy of the police report OR
 ✓ A copy of the court outcome if the criminal was identified and went to court OR
 ✓ A copy of your medical records if you were injured in the crime (and one of the above)

✓ It's not a requirement, but it's best to have a psychological report on the trauma you experienced. The more trauma you can prove you experienced (such as not being able to sleep, go outdoors, or work), the better.

With one or more of the above documents, go to an Immigration Expert and discuss how you might qualify for a U-Visa. Immigration Services issues 10,000 U-Visas every year. It takes about three years to receive a U-Visa. You will have to prove that you have been a good person, have not committed any serious crimes, and will be physically present in the United States for the next three years. Three years after receiving your U-Visa, you can apply for permanent residency and eventually receive a green card.

If your last entry was without inspection (undocumented), you would need to apply for **Advance Permission to Enter as a Nonimmigrant (form I-192.)** This waiver is discretionary. That means an immigration officer makes the final decision on the waiver.

Other family members that may qualify when you apply for a U-Visa:
1) If you are under the age of 21, your parents and unmarried siblings under age 18 may qualify.
2) If you are over the age of 21, only your spouse and children may qualify.

There is no limit on the number of visas available for dependent family members. However, this may change as the Trump administration has asked the government to change the rules and limit family members who can qualify.

The Process: Go to a non-profit organization or Immigration Expert, as the steps are complicated. You need the items mentioned above, and your Immigration Expert will process the application. Your Immigration Expert will have to obtain a **U-Cert** which must be signed by the law enforcement agency or District Attorney involved with the crime. Once you have received the signed U-Cert, you must file the U-Visa application (**I-918**) within six months of the signature date on the U-Cert.

Work Permit/EAD Card: If you have been the victim of a crime on United States soil, you should include **two** work permit (**I-765**) applications with your U-Visa Application (**I-918**). Obtaining a U-Visa may take a few years. Immigration Services will review your application and place you on the "approved" waiting list. **If you have completed the two work permit (I-765) applications, they will issue you a two-year EAD card** for the waiting period. Once your U-Visa is approved, you will receive a work permit for the duration of the U-Visa (three years).

Filing Fees: There is no filing fee for the U-Visa (**I-918**). Two-year EAD card (**I-765**) $820. Your Immigration Expert will charge additional fees for their services. Su Experto en Inmigración le cobrará tarifas adicionales por sus servicios

If you entered without inspection (undocumented), you must fill out the **Application for Advance Permission to Enter as a Nonimmigrant (I-192) for $930.** If you do not have the money, you can ask your Immigration Expert for a fee waiver.

I Was Brought to the U.S. and Forced into the Sex Industry or Forced Labor (T-Visa)

The T-Visa (Application for T Nonimmigrant Status, form **I-914**) is for people who were brought to the United States either with or without legal documentation and were forced to work against their will. This includes being forced into the sex industry, involuntary labor, or servant work with little or no pay. Immigration Services issues 5,000 T-Visas every year. Victims who obtain a T-Visa can bring in close family members.

Signs you are a victim of trafficking:
- ✓ You are forced to perform sex or do service work against your will
- ✓ You are physically present in the United States and were brought here with a promise of another job
- ✓ You are not allowed to leave your job
- ✓ Your employer gives you little or no money for your work
- ✓ You are forced to sleep and eat where you work
- ✓ You are in debt to your employer
- ✓ When you arrived, they took away your passport and any identification
- ✓ They threaten to harm your family back home if you try to escape

If someone forced you into performing sex or forced you into labor under controlled conditions, contact the National Human Trafficking Hotline for free at 1-888-373-7888. This organization is completely confidential and will not report you to your employer or **ICE**. They can tell you where to go or even send people to help you and the others working there.

Individual Requirements:

- ✓ You must be able to describe your experience to law officials, which will result in the investigation and possible arrest of your employers. The people at the National Human Trafficking Hotline will help you with this.
- ✓ You must still reside in the United States.
- ✓ You must have been brought here against your will OR under a false promise, and then been forced into the sex industry, involuntary labor, or servant work.
- ✓ You must prove you would experience extreme hardship if deported back to your home country (see *Chapter Five*).
- ✓ You must be able to demonstrate that you have been a good person and have not committed any serious crimes.

Remember, it is important to communicate that you were brought to the United States and forced to perform a service against your will. You will not qualify if you previously did the same work in your home country. For example, if you worked in the sex industry in your home country, then you could not get a T-Visa for working in the sex industry in the United States.

You will also have to demonstrate that you are a person of good moral character. If you were forced to commit crimes, explain that you did so only under force. Ask the **National Human Trafficking Hotline** for a local non-profit immigration service. They will be able to assist with your legal needs.

Even if you managed to escape from your employer and you are now working elsewhere without documentation in the United States, you could still qualify for a T-Visa. It is important to find an Immigration Expert to help you or call the National Human Trafficking Hotline.

The Process: The first step is to get the National Human Trafficking Hotline involved. It is essential that they help you find a local non-profit immigration organization or an Immigration Expert to help you. You will need to complete several forms. If you want to include any immediate family members, you will need to use a separate form.

You will have to provide evidence proving you helped law enforcement officials in the case against your former employer. You will need to complete the T-Visa (**I-914**). Or, you can provide other types of proof such as court documents, police reports, news articles, letters on your behalf from others involved, and other evidence.

If brought to the United States without documentation, you will also need to demonstrate that you have a credible fear of being harmed if returned to your home country. See *Chapter Four* and read what that means and how to develop your story.

If you entered without inspection (undocumented), you must fill out the **Application for Advance Permission to Enter as a Nonimmigrant (I-192).** You would skip this if you were brought here with a visa. Three years after receiving your T-Visa, you may qualify for a green card.

Work Permit/EAD Card: When Immigration Services grants you your T-Visa, you will automatically receive the employment document (EAD card). This process can take three to five months depending on your case.

Filing fees: There is no filing fee for the T-Visa (**I-914**). Also, it's easy to receive a filing fee waiver for any other forms when connected to a T-Visa. Your Immigration Expert will charge additional fees for their services.

I Am a Witness to or Know of Serious Crimes Committed by Gangs, the Cartel, Terrorists, or Others in the U.S. (S-Visa)

The S-Visa (Green Card for an Informant S Nonimmigrant) is for people who can be a witness or informant for law enforcement. There are only 250 S-Visas issued per year. The S-Visa is designed for people who can help stop criminal organizations (200 visas) or can help stop terrorist groups (50 visas) from committing crimes in the United States. If you are a witness to a serious crime that can lead to arrests, you may qualify. For example, if someone forced you to bring drugs over the border, or if you discovered a criminal act in the United States and you have evidence that could lead the police to find and arrest the criminals, you may be able to use this to obtain an S-Visa. **However, before you report this, we highly suggest you contact an Immigration Expert and seek their advice.**

Individual Requirements:
To obtain an S-Visa, you must have information relating to a crime that has happened or is about to happen. You must be willing to provide the information to the police and help them when they ask. The petitioner (the person who files your S-Visa application) MUST be an officer from the federal or state police or a lawyer from the U.S. Attorney's Office. **We highly suggest you use an Immigration Expert for the process. They can contact the police on your behalf.** Once you have done your part (you helped in the arrest of the criminal), you will begin by asking the police to complete the application.

The Process:
- ✓ **Step One:** File the **Interagency Alien Witness and Informant Record (form I-854).** An officer from the federal or state police or a lawyer from the U.S. Attorney's Office must fill out and sign this form. You

will need to provide evidence that you helped in identifying the criminal(s). Also, you must disclose the reasons you are undocumented in the U.S., as well as any crimes you have committed.

✓ **Step Two:** After your **I-854** is approved, you must then file the **Application to Adjust Status (form I-485).** At that time, you can also apply for your work permit.

Work Permit/EAD Card: After your **I-854** is approved, you can then file for your Application to Adjust Status (**I-485**) along with your application for a work permit (**I-765**). Your work permit will take about three months. While you wait for the green card, you will be allowed to work.

Filing Fees: There is no filing fee for the S-Visa. Green Card $1440. Biometrics $85.

I Am Homeless in the U.S., under the Age of 18, and Have Lost My Parents or Guardians (SIJS)

If you are under the age of 18 and you are homeless because your parents have abandoned you or you have been a victim of abuse, the Special Immigrant Juvenile Status may be an option for you.

Special Immigrant Juvenile Status (SIJS) is for undocumented people under the age of 18, but you may still qualify if you are under 21. The best thing you can do is call the **National Center for Homeless Education at 1-800-786-2929**. It is free to call. This organization can help you find quick shelter and local resources for legal assistance. They will not report you to ICE.

Questions to Consider:
- ✓ Have you been mentally, physically, or sexually abused by a parent, step-parent, or legal guardian, which caused you to run away from home?
- ✓ Have you been the victim of a serious crime? This may include domestic violence, being forced into servitude or hard labor with little or no pay or having to perform sexual acts on others.
- ✓ Do you come from a country that has experienced a civil war, natural disaster, or out-of-control gangs? If forced to return to your home country, do you fear persecution because of your race or religion?

In all cases, you will have to demonstrate that you have been a good person, have not committed any serious crimes, and have a desire to go to school and work in the United States. You can call the telephone number above and ask for assistance. Or, you can contact a non-profit legal aid organization.

You should be aware that if you have committed any serious crimes while on United States soil, it could affect your application. It is best to have a clean record. Be sure to tell the person who helps with your application everything from your past.

Individual Requirements:
- ✓ You must be under the age of 21 when you file your application
- ✓ You must never have been married
- ✓ You must currently be living in the United States
- ✓ You must have a valid juvenile court order that says you cannot be united with your parents or foster parents.
- ✓ You must demonstrate that it is not in your best interest to return to your home country because you have no support structure or because the government-supported gangs would try to recruit you.

The Process: To apply for SIJS you must file the following forms and supporting documentation with Immigration Services:
- ✓ Petition for Special Immigrant Juvenile Status (**I-360**)
- ✓ Application to Adjust Status (**I-485**)
- ✓ Evidence of your age such as a valid passport, birth certificate, or other age identification
- ✓ A valid juvenile court order that says your parents or legal guardians abandoned you or you can no longer live with them. A local non-profit legal assistance aid organization will help you obtain this if you do not have the document.

Once you submit these documents, you will receive a receipt notice. A little later you will receive a second notice for **biometrics** (fingerprint notice). This letter will give you a time and place where you will go to have your fingerprints and photo taken. You must do this as part of the application.

The last document is the Report of Medical Examination and Vaccination Record (**I-693**). Normally you can provide this at the same time as your application, but some processing centers take longer than a year. It's best to know how long your application will take up front and do everything together. However, the medical examination is only good for a year.

NOTE: When you apply for your SIJS and green card, you will NOT be required to contact the individual or family members who abused, abandoned, or neglected you.

WARNING: If you receive SIJS, your parents or family who abandoned you will NEVER be able obtain a legal status through you even if you become a citizen.

Immigration Services (**USCIS**) generally takes about six months to decide on your application. If you did not submit enough information, they would send you a **Request for Evidence.** That will stop the process and delay your application.

Work Permit/EAD Card: When you apply for your visa, you can simultaneously apply for your green card. You also attach the application for your work permit/EAD card (**I-765**).

Filing Fees: There is no filing fee for the Special Immigrant Juvenile Status (**I-360**). Green Card/Application to Register Permanent Residence or Adjust Status (**I-485**) $1,140. However, it is possible to have fees waived on the initial application.

I Have No Way to Become Documented at This Time. What Do I Do?

This is the case if none of the previous options have applied to you, you have no credible fear story, and the only reason you are in the U.S. is economic (seeking a better life) or to be with family. If you do not have a good story, chances are ICE will deport you if they catch up with you.

You likely have little chance to stay if:
- ✓ You have committed multiple crimes in the United States and have no story of fear if returned to your home country
- ✓ Police have connected you with any serious gangs, such as MS-13
- ✓ The only reason you are in the United States is to seek a better life
- ✓ You came here because you wanted to be with other family members
- ✓ You have multiple re-entries and no credible story of fear in your home country
- ✓ You have thoroughly read this chapter, and you do not qualify for any of the options

If Immigration Services knows you are here and has issued a deportation order: It all depends on you. The letter will specify the date you must leave the country. It is normally 30 days from the date of the letter. If you choose to ignore a deportation order, you could work in the United States undocumented until the day they find and arrest you. Read *Chapter Nine* on how to avoid ICE.

Do not break any laws and be careful when in public. Then

save all the money you can. If you are caught and deported, Immigration Services could bar you from legally entering the United States for ten years to life. We predict that once Trump has left office, sanity will return to the United States Government, and new laws will be passed. If your desire is to one day work legally in the United States, you may consider voluntary departure.

Keep in mind that even if you end up back in your home country and you have a new reason to apply again, you can use the **Application for Permission to Reapply for Admission into the United States After Deportation or Removal (I-212)** to return legally. Know that these are hard to obtain, but with enough documentation and proof, it is possible.

Voluntary Departure: If Immigration Services knows you are here and you are in removal proceedings, consider voluntary departure. Perhaps you have a weak argument, and you know eventually you will lose. You can continue to appeal your case to higher courts, but this can be expensive. You can tell the courts that if denied, you would accept voluntary departure.

This option offers some benefits:

- ✓ If you voluntarily depart on the agreed date, you may not be subject to the three-year or ten-year bar from re-entering the U.S. For example, once you have a convincing reason to re-enter, you could begin the process of applying for a visa and not have to wait out the time.
- ✓ When speaking to the judge, you can extend your departure date to 60 or even 120 days to give you time to sell off assets and organize your belongings before your departure.

It is important to note that voluntary departure is the decision of the judge. If you have committed serious crimes such as falsifying documents or the judge feels you are a threat to society, you will not qualify. You must also prove you can pay for your ticket back to your home country.

If Immigration Services does not know you are here:
You have read this entire chapter, and you do not qualify for any of the options. You cannot sleep at night, and you are afraid to go out during the day because of what President Trump is doing to immigrants. You know the only reason you came to the United States was to seek a better life, and you do not have a good argument for asylum. If this describes you, you have two options:

1) **Return to your home country:** Only consider this if you have no record of you being here and you find that living in the United States now is too hostile for undocumented people. Consider waiting to re-enter until the Trump government and their anti-immigrant policies have ended.

2) **Read the rest of this book:** Do what you have been doing. Remember, an estimated 11 million undocumented people live in the United States. If you learn to lay low, you can survive while waiting for the Trump government and anti-immigrant policies to end. With a little luck, Congress will pass reasonable laws that allow you to stay in the United States with documentation. The choice is up to you.

STEP THREE:
Read *Chapter Four* and pay attention to what your story must contain for your application to be successful. Carefully recall your experience in your home country for an Asylum Application or learn how to prove hardship in a Family or Marriage Application.

<u>Chapter Four</u>

Developing Your Story

"I had always hoped that this land might become a safe and agreeable Asylum to the virtuous and persecuted part of mankind, to whatever nation they might belong." –George Washington

----

What You Will Learn:
- ✓ How to develop your asylum story
- ✓ What "extreme hardship" means to Immigration Services
- ✓ What it means to have "good moral character"
- ✓ How to convince Immigration Services to accept your Asylum Application if you have been here past the one-year deadline

Words to Know:

Discrimination: When people harm you or are unfair to you because of where you come from, how you look, your religion, or your sexual orientation

Condemn: When someone expresses their negative feelings about you in public or private

Introduction

When undocumented immigrants fail to prove their case, it is often because they do not know how the system works. This chapter is about convincing officials why you should be allowed to stay in the United States. Your chances depend on the following:

- ✓ Is your asylum story believable? (for Asylum, Withholding of Removal, or CAT)
- ✓ Can your legal U.S. sponsor survive financially and emotionally if you are deported, or would they experience hardship? (for Family Petition, Marriage Petition, or Ten-Year Cancellation of Removal)
- ✓ Have you been a good person while living in the United States? (for all applications except CAT and Withholding of Removal)

Countless people who had a true asylum story failed to tell it properly. They were deported back to their home country only to end up assaulted or killed. Or, they were deported because they failed to convince Immigration Services of the extreme hardship their family would go through if they were separated.

TRUE ASYLUM STORY: A woman named Elena from Honduras fled to the United States because MS-13 had murdered two of her brothers and were pressuring her to hide gang money in banks under her name. She refused to help, and the gang went after her. She fled to the United States. After a few years working undocumented, she was caught in a raid and arrested. Then she applied for asylum. The asylum officer was not convinced. She had a second chance in court. The judge asked one question: "Did you move to any other city in Honduras before coming to the United States?" She said no. She did not convince the judge that she tried hard enough to survive elsewhere in her country before going to the United States. The judge denied her application. Deported back to Honduras, the gang then assaulted her.

If Elena was prepared: The judge may have allowed Elena to stay if she had explained that it made no difference where she lived within her country because Honduras is about the size of the state of Georgia. It would be easy for the gang to find her. Furthermore, had she presented evidence with newspaper articles of what has happened to others, proof of her murdered brothers, and a reasonable argument that the same thing would happen to her regardless of which city she lived in within Honduras, she may have had a chance.

NOTE: This book will not teach you how to lie. What you say to a court or immigration officer is up to you. If you are caught lying, or changing your story, you will likely be deported and barred from entering the U.S. for ten years to life.

Part One: Developing Your Story (Asylum, UAC, Withholding of Removal, and CAT)

If your application is not about these, skip to Part Two.

The United States recognizes the right of asylum for people. You can only request asylum if you are physically in the United States or at the border. However, your story must be convincing and consistent (cannot change). And it must **NOT be because you are seeking a better life or want to live with your family.** Your story must convince officials that if you are returned to your home country, a significant possibility exists that you will be tortured, beaten, or killed.

You must have a story of fear and this story must be consistent.

In Trump's America, **ICE** looks for any reason to deport you and will use the slightest excuse to do so. You must have a story that they cannot deny. One good thing about asylum is that you do not have to have proof of your story. Testimony and evidence of country conditions is often enough.

> **TRUE ASYLUM STORY:** In El Salvador, Erica had been abused by her stepfather since she was five years old. Finally, at the age of 18 she managed to run away from home and make her way to the United States. For years she was hiding until one day, ICE arrested her. She found a good lawyer who sent her to a psychologist. After a few sessions, the psychologist developed a report about her trauma, stating that the 12 years of abuse had left her so traumatized that she needed care which was not available in El Salvador.

Erica was prepared: The psychologist report on her trauma, plus, evidence about conditions in her home country, convinced the immigration judge the story was credible. Her case was approved.

> **One way to support your story is to have a psychologist develop a report of your mental condition. The report can be used in court or, even better, the psychologist can testify on your behalf.**

What is your story?

> **NOTE:** In June of 2018, the Trump government announced that a story using gangs or abusive spouses will no longer qualify as a credible story unless it was tied to your country's government. If possible, your story should be tied to in-country laws that limit the rights of women (for example) or the refusal of the government (police) to protect you from gangs. We believe this rule will be eventually over-ruled by a U.S. Court.

You will not qualify if you only say that you came to the United States because as a child, a relative abused you. The judge would respond that now you are an adult and you can protect yourself. Your story must come from your experience of the past AND it must also convince an immigration officer or judge that if you were to return, anywhere in your country, the trauma would more than likely happen again. You could also explain that you were so traumatized by your experience, you could not survive on your own there, and/or you need ongoing treatment which is not available there. Finally, your story must be believable.

No single standard determines if you are in fear for your life. It is the combination of your entire story and evidence of conditions in your home country that can be tied to your experience. Your story must include one or more of the following from the **Five Protected Grounds:**

1) Were you harmed because of **your race (tribe or minority group of people)**? Being oppressed is not enough.
2) Did people **discriminate against you (threatened, harmed, or rejected you)** because of your **religion**?
3) Did people want to harm you because you or a close family member is an outspoken person or part of a **political party**?
4) Was your **gender or sexual orientation** routinely discriminated against (woman, gay, lesbian)?
5) Did people condemn you because you are associated with a **particular social group**? See the list of social group examples.

In law, these are called the **five protected grounds.** You may think that your story does not fit any. Making a successful argument is where a good Immigration Expert can help you. A married woman is considered a "member of a social group" for example. A few examples of "social groups" that can qualify include:

✓ Gay, lesbian, or transgender
✓ Doctor, journalist, public official, or police officer
✓ DACA or children living in the United States most of their life who are "Americanized"
✓ Street Children
✓ Escaped from a gang (running from a gang recruiter or girlfriend of a gang member)
✓ In fear of harm from a rival gang

Evidence for your story: Do you have written statements from family or people in your home country who have witnessed your experience? An Immigration Expert also knows how to do research and find evidence about country conditions. Also, consider talking to a psychologist. In a few sessions, they can understand your mental condition and determine any long-term damage your trauma caused, as well as what might happen if you return.

A report from a qualified psychologist can be valuable to your case. Having them testify is even better.

Examples of evidence:
- ✓ Visible scars on your body or your child's body
- ✓ Pictures of wounds inflicted on you by someone in your home country
- ✓ Proof that your home country government is unwilling or unable to help you (newspaper articles and statements from friends)
- ✓ Recent news articles on the conditions in your country (6-8 articles)
- ✓ Research or studies from credible organizations about the conditions of your country
- ✓ Police reports of an incident that you or a family member was involved in
- ✓ Receipts or records of you being in the hospital because of the incident
- ✓ Letters from people in your home country explaining the dangers of living there
- ✓ Psychologist reports from here in the United States stating your mental condition
- ✓ Letters of threats from people in your home country

Remember, all evidence you use in court MUST be in English, and the translation must be certified. Most of your story is based on personal testimony, and it must be consistent.

Developing your story: Do not make up your story in front of the immigration officer or judge. BE PREPARED. Before you go to court, think about your experience in detail and then write it down. Details and consistency are important. Often Immigration Services will ask you the same question in different ways to trick you. It is very important to keep your story the same.

IMPORTANT: If you told your story to an immigration officer and now you must tell it to a judge in court, your story cannot change. You can add detail to the original story, but you cannot change any detail.

Your story does not have to be about you. It can also be about family members in your application such as your children, siblings, or spouse. This would help prove your region is dangerous and your family is a target.

What your story should contain:
- ✓ When did the threat or abuse happen?
- ✓ Where did it happen?
- ✓ Why did they do it?
- ✓ Who else was involved?
- ✓ What happened to you or to your family member?
- ✓ Who harmed you? Were they a person of the law, a public official, a relative, a gang member?
- ✓ Were you beaten, threatened, raped, or tortured?
- ✓ Did they use guns or other kinds of weapons?
- ✓ Was a friend or someone you know harmed or killed in your home country who you could tie into your story?
- ✓ Did you try to contact the police? If so, what happened? If not, why not?
- ✓ And, most importantly, if returned, what would happen to you?

The immigration officer or judge will ask why you cannot live somewhere else in your country. You can respond by saying that you have no family network and it would be impossible to survive. You must prove the conditions are the same in all cities in your country and your life would be in danger regardless of where you live in your country.

Your story must include that you had to go to the United States because there were no other options and you and your family members' lives are in danger. Going to the United States was your only option.

Describe the conditions in your country. Describe how the police or even the government officials treat the people. The story cannot be about poverty or lack of jobs.

What your story should NOT contain:

- ✓ It should never be about "seeking a better life" because there are no opportunities in your country.
- ✓ It should never be because "my family lives in the United States."
- ✓ It should never be inconsistent. If you provided a written statement of your story, make sure your verbal story is the same.
- ✓ It should never involve something that is not scientifically provable, such as magic, superstitions, aliens, supernatural powers, and so on.

NOTE: Immigration Services will deport you if your reason for coming to the United States is to seek a better life. Your reason must be fear for your life if returned to your home country.

When you tell your story to the judge or interviewer:
We go into this in more detail in *Chapter Five*, Representing Yourself in Court. It is extremely important that your story comes from your heart. Cry and express fear if possible.

When you tell it, do so with emotion as if you were there experiencing it all over again, be certain of the details, and make sure they do not change. A good Immigration Expert will help you.

Be prepared. If you are applying for **Affirmative Asylum,** an immigration officer will interview you. They will ask you 75-100 questions. Many of these questions will be the same but asked differently

The conclusion of your story must be that you fear for your life if returned to your home country and you considered ALL options before coming to the United States.

T-Visa Story Only

T-Visa: (for victims of trafficking) should be about what might happen to you if you are returned to your home country. Examples are:
- ✓ I was unknowingly sold off by my parents into servitude. If I were to return, my family and entire community will reject me for fear the smugglers will come after me again.
- ✓ If the smugglers find me back in my home country, I would be in fear or my life.
- ✓ Because I was forced into the sex industry, if I were to return to my country the community will reject me for what I was forced to do.

Part Two: Proving "Extreme Hardship"

If you entered the United States without documentation and want to become documented, the process is complicated. Part of this process is to demonstrate that if you are separated from your legal family in the United States, they will experience extreme hardship.

"**Extreme hardship**" is based on a combination of factors. Immigration Services determines your eligibility by totaling the factors listed below:

- ✓ **Family Ties in the United States:** How many children do you have who are U.S. citizens, and what are their ages? Are you supporting elderly relatives of yours or your spouse? How long have you been married to your U.S. citizen spouse? Did your spouse spend any time in the military? How long have you lived in the United States?
- ✓ **Social and Cultural Impact:** What connections does your citizen spouse have in the United States? Would there be cultural challenges if your spouse had to move from the United States to your home country? Would there be difficulty affording travel between the two countries to maintain relationships?
- ✓ **Economic Impact:** This is a major factor in the decision. Do you have evidence that you provide the primary income in the family and that your deportation would likely result in your legal spouse having to rely on public financial assistance? If deported, what is the economic impact on your citizen spouse and family? Would your spouse be able to provide for the family without public assistance?
- ✓ **Health Conditions and Care:** What are the health conditions of your legal resident family? What impact

would the separation of the family have socially and financially? Do any of your children or your spouse have mental or physical conditions that need constant attention? Does this prevent your spouse from working full time or at all? Do any of your legal close family members have psychological reports of anxiety, depression, or other mental illnesses? You will need medical records for proof.

✓ **Separation Effect:** If you are deported, how would your family be impacted?

✓ **Country Conditions:** What are the economic, political, and legal conditions of your country? Does the U.S. Department of State list your home country as dangerous? Have there been any severe environmental problems recently?

Proving extreme hardship is about organizing your evidence and developing your story about how your spouse and/or parents would go through extreme hardship if you were separated. Review the items we listed above. The more of these you can include in your story, the better. Remember, the officer or judge will evaluate your case in its entirety. Provide all the documents you can.

Part Three: Proving "Good Moral Character"

Having good moral character means you follow written and societal laws, and you contribute in some way to your community. A judge will decide your future based on the evidence, how you support your legal family, and who you are as a person.

For legal purposes, a person with good moral character is one who follows the rules, pays their taxes, has a good job, and perhaps goes to church. In other words, they live like an average U.S. citizen.

A judge or immigration officer will determine your moral character based on the following:

- ✓ Do you have a police record? Your case will be difficult if you have multiple serious misdemeanor charges or a felony charge.
- ✓ If you committed any crimes, have you been responsible since then? Can you obtain a letter of recommendation from your parole officer?
- ✓ Do you have any formal education? Are you trying to learn English?
- ✓ How long have you worked at your present job? How many jobs have you had in the past? The longer you have been at your job, the better. Can you obtain a letter of recommendation from your boss?
- ✓ Can you prove you pay taxes and file your tax returns every year? Even if you used a fake Social Security number, provide copies of tax returns.
- ✓ Do you volunteer your time for any organization? Do you have any certificates of recognition? Can you obtain letters of support from others?

✓ Do you attend church on a regular basis? Can you obtain a letter of recommendation from your pastor?
✓ How long have you lived in the United States? The longer, the better.

Ask your friends for letters of recommendation. They will need to include their names and addresses on the letter. You cannot have too many letters. And if you committed a crime in the past, the more letters that demonstrate you are a changed person, the better.

Part Four: Convincing Immigration Services to Accept your Asylum Application If You Have Been in the United States for More Than a Year

The law says that you have one year to apply for asylum after entering the country. However, under what Immigration Services calls "Extraordinary Circumstances," you can still apply after the one-year deadline. You must have a convincing reason prepared before you apply to Immigration Services.

An application could be accepted past the one-year deadline if:
- ✓ Conditions in your country have changed
- ✓ You were dealing with trauma or debilitating conditions
- ✓ You were included as a dependent in someone else's application, but the application was denied
- ✓ There were problems in your life beyond your control that prevented you from applying within the first year (must detail the problems)
- ✓ You were seriously ill or physically disabled
- ✓ You were dealing with a mental condition
- ✓ You had a bad lawyer or notary that delayed your application
- ✓ Your Immigration Expert or a member of your immediate family experienced serious illness, incapacity, or death

If you have waited more than a year after entering the U.S. to file your Asylum Application, you need to have a good story why you did not file on time. Use these reasons to organize your story. Your Immigration Expert or a non-profit legal aid organization can help you.

<u>Chapter Five</u>

Representing Yourself in Court or at an Interview

"We are a nation of immigrants. We are the children and grandchildren and great-grandchildren of the ones who wanted a better life, the driven ones, the ones who woke up at night hearing that voice telling them that life in that place called America could be better." –Mitt Romney

----

What You Will Learn:
- ✓ What a Notice to Appear (NTA) is
- ✓ How the master hearing (MH) works
- ✓ How the individual hearing (IH) works
- ✓ How the appeal process works
- ✓ What to expect at an Affirmative Asylum/UAC interview
- ✓ What to expect at a Marriage/Family Petition interview
- ✓ What to expect at a consular interview in your home country

Words to Know:

Appeal: To apply to a higher court to reverse the decision of a lower court

Objection: Expressing your disagreement with a piece of evidence or the statement of the opposing side in court

Respondent: The accused person

Cross-Examine: To ask questions of the opposing person and argue whether their statement is true

Brief: A legal document that is presented to a court stating why a person in a case should win

Prosecutor/ICE Lawyer: The person responsible for representing the government in a trial

Introduction

Whether you are a United States citizen or an undocumented immigrant, being interviewed or defending yourself can be one of the most difficult undertakings in your life. When English is not your first language and you do not understand the United States legal system, representing yourself is even more difficult.

WARNING: We wrote this chapter for those with NO OTHER OPTION. Immigrants who represent themselves in court often fail. If possible, use an Immigration Expert.

Reasons why you may fail if you represent yourself:
- ✓ **Not understanding what is happening in court:** More than likely English is your second language. You do not understand the legal language and how to respond during the court process.
- ✓ **The ICE lawyer knows more than you do about the law:** The court hearing will be you versus an ICE immigration lawyer. The lawyer knows the law and has heard hundreds of cases like yours. Their job is to convince the judge that you are lying and that they should deport you. You have not done this before and must defend yourself against the lawyer.
- ✓ **You did not bring any supporting evidence:** Immigration courts rely on a combination of testimony and documentary evidence. Evidence can be a collection of news articles, police reports, pictures, and psychological studies for example, which you give the courts to help prove your case. Having physical evidence translated into English is important for your case.

We cannot state enough the importance of hiring an experienced Immigration Expert. All research has found that your chances of winning your case are much better with an Immigration Expert than if you try to defend your case yourself.

For those who have no choice but to represent themselves, this chapter will cover the following:

Part One: Representing Yourself in Court Hearings (for Removal Proceedings)

The two types of court hearings:
- ✓ **Master Hearing (MH)** Usually a short hearing, five to ten minutes. You may appear at more than one type of Master Hearing
- ✓ **Individual Hearing (IH)** Usually one to six hours or longer

Part Two: Representing Yourself in Immigration Interviews

The three most common interviews with immigration officers:
- ✓ Affirmative Asylum and UAC
- ✓ Green card based on Marriage Petition or Family Petition
- ✓ **Consular interview** at a U.S. Consulate in your home country

The courts have specific procedures on how to act, how to submit evidence, how to include witnesses, and how to communicate with the judge or immigration officer. This chapter offers an overview of how to defend yourself.

UNLESS YOU HAVE NO OTHER OPTIONS, DO NOT TRY TO DO THIS ALONE. USING AN IMMIGRATION EXPERT WILL DRASTICALLY IMPROVE YOUR CHANCES OF SUCCESS. IF YOU DO THIS ON YOUR OWN AND YOU FAIL, APPEAL AND THEN FIND AN IMMIGRATION LAWYER.

Part One: Representing Yourself in Court

Court hearings are usually the last step in an application process before you are either formally approved or denied legal residency in the United States. Fortunately, if you do not like the judge's decision, the United States justice system has an appeal process that allows you to appeal to a higher court (three possible appeals). This is important because not all judges see the law the same way. For example, according to Reuters' analysis of data from the Executive Office of Immigration Review, if you apply for asylum in the southeast area of the United States, your chances of success are 10-20%. If you apply for asylum in the western part of the United States, your chances are as high as 60-75%.

Your Notice to Appear: A court process begins with a "**Notice to Appear**" or **NTA.** You will receive the NTA in the mail, or it will be given to you if you are in detention. The NTA will give you two important points of information:

- ✓ **The charges against you**: The NTA will state that the government has charged you with being in the United States without authorization (no documentation). It may also include other charges. You must understand the charges because your defense is about proving why you are not guilty of these charges.

✓ **Your court date**: Most of the time the NTA document will have your court date. If you receive an NTA without a court date, Immigration Services will send you a future document with that date. You can also call 1-800-898-7180 and enter your **A-Number** (on your NTA). A recording will give you the assigned court date.

What happens if I ignore the NTA and skip the court date?
If you miss your court date, you could lose any chance of becoming documented. The judge will issue a deportation order. If ICE knows where you live, you can expect a knock on your door soon, and ICE will arrest everyone in your home or work who is undocumented. To avoid being detained, read *Chapter Nine*. It is important to realize that skipping your court date could end your chances of becoming documented.

The NTA is usually the first document a lawyer asks for when they represent you in court. It tells them what they must do to defend you and how much time they have.

We cannot go into detail on how to submit your documents. If you are doing this on your own, we highly suggest you seek some professional advice from a non-profit legal aid organization. Remember, everything you submit must be in English. Here are some tips to keep in mind:

1) **Dress nicely:** You want to do whatever it takes to please the court and demonstrate that you take this seriously. The best option is a suit and tie or a conservative dress. If you do not have that, at least wear something that is clean. Do not come in your work clothes.

2) **Do not bring disruptions:** Do not bring your children. Do not bring any food or drinks. You do not want to bring anything that can be disruptive in the court.

3) **Arrive early:** It is better to arrive an hour early than five minutes late. We know of people who arrived at the court but ended up in the wrong building or courtroom, or who had a delay due to traffic and were late. The court will not wait for you. When at your designated courtroom, you will need to sign in. Normally you will find the paper on the wall near the courtroom door. Ask people around you for the right procedure.

4) **Speak some English if you can:** Demonstrate to the judge that you are trying to learn English. However, unless you are fluent, only say one or two lines in English and then say you would prefer to use your native language so you do not miss anything. Be sure to tell the court ahead of time that you will need an interpreter.

5) **Be prepared:** If you are submitting documents to the court, have them organized in a way that is easy to use while you give your story. If you brought any witnesses, they should sit in the benches behind you.

NOTE: By law, the hearing cannot proceed unless you have an interpreter for your language.

ICE Prosecution Lawyer: This is the person who will try to convince the judge you are guilty and should be sent back to your home country. They have years of experience in court. Keep in mind though, the ICE lawyer likely has not seen your case until the last few hours. You have months to prepare.

The Hearings

The Master Hearing (MH)

The master hearing is short, usually five to ten minutes at most. It is to establish how you wish to plead in your case (guilty or not guilty), and to set a date to have you case organized by the respondent (you) will ask for time to find a lawyer (if necessary).

You or your Immigration Expert will ask for more time to prepare the case or enter pleadings and submit an Asylum Application (if necessary). We recommend 90-120 days. The date will be set for the final hearing if there are no outstanding issues. You may receive the final hearing date in writing.

You will not need to provide any evidence supporting your case at this hearing, but you must submit your application (Asylum, 42B, or others). The main purpose is for you to admit or deny the allegations listed on the **Notice to Appear (NTA)**. You are the "respondent." Depending on your case, there may be more than one master hearing before your individual hearing.

If you do not feel comfortable speaking English, don't. You do not want to miss anything. If you do not speak English and you attend without an Immigration Expert, inform the court beforehand of the language you speak. They will make an interpreter available. Do not try to communicate in a language you are not completely comfortable speaking. If no interpreter is available, the judge will set a new court date. You want to get an interpreter because any miscommunication or confusion over what you say might cause the judge to rule against you.

The hearing will begin with the judge asking you for your

personal information such as name, address, native language, and perhaps other languages you are fluent in. Then, the judge will read the charges against you as listed on your NTA. Be sure to tell the judge if anything is inaccurate on the NTA.

If you intend to stay in the United States, deny the charges on the NTA. Again, submit your application before or at the master hearing. Make two extra copies of your application: one for the ICE lawyer and one for yourself. The original goes to the court. At that point, tell the judge you are seeking asylum, Withholding of Removal, or Cancellation of Removal. Make sure you have read **Chapter Three** to know which status you are requesting. If you are claiming asylum, the judge will ask you to name your home country. You must say there is nowhere in your home country you would feel safe returning to. The very reason you are applying for asylum is that you are afraid to return to your home country. Regardless, the judge will write down your home country as part of the procedure.

At the end of the hearing, the judge will set your next court date(s). If you are in detention, they may set another master hearing for your **bond** (set amount paid to the government in return for your release) and then for your individual hearing.

You want to give yourself plenty of time before the individual hearing to prepare your story. If you found this event overwhelming, find an Immigration Expert to help you.

At the end of the hearing, the court will give you a written notice stating the date of your next hearing.

The Individual Hearing (IH)
  - ✓ All supporting documents are due 15-30 days before the court hearing.

✓ All evidence and testimonies are presented at this hearing.

✓ The judge can make a decision either on that day or later in a written decision.

The individual hearing is the all-important hearing that determines if you will be allowed to stay in the United States. The hearing may last two to six hours or perhaps even longer. It depends on how much evidence you wish to review and how many witnesses are testifying in your defense.

Remember, every case is different, including yours. Keep in mind:

✓ If you have been in the United States for more than a year and are only now applying for asylum, you will have to give a good reason why you did not apply before the one-year deadline.

✓ If you have committed any criminal offenses such as drunk driving or domestic violence, you will have to explain them. You cannot hide them because the ICE lawyer will have copies of your criminal record.

✓ If you have re-entered the United States more than once, you will have to explain why. If this is the case, you likely can only apply for Withholding of Removal.

✓ If your NTA paper lists any other charges, you will have to explain them.

If you have hired an Immigration Expert, they will have developed a **brief** which is a document arguing why your case should be approved based on past cases similar to yours. It is not necessary to provide a legal brief, but it does help greatly in convincing the judge that you should stay.

You will need to give the court copies of any evidence you want to include and a list of any witnesses. You will need to submit these items 15-30 days prior to your hearing (depending on the judge). See **Chapter five**.

Regardless of the outcome of your case, you will **NOT** be arrested at the courthouse. You will be able to go home to your family. ICE will not detain you.

The Day of Your Hearing
To see what the day of your hearing may look like, go to the **Useful Websites** section of this book and look for the web address that links to a YouTube video on court procedures. It will give you an idea of what will happen at your court hearing.

The Individual Hearing (IH) Court Process
In the courtroom, there will be two tables. You will sit at one, and the ICE lawyer will sit at the other. The judge may already be sitting. If not, stand up when the judge arrives and wait to sit down until they are seated. If you are unsure, do what the ICE lawyer does.

First, the judge will read the charges listed on your Notice to Appear letter. You will have a chance to correct anything that may have changed since your master hearing, such as a new address. Also, the judge will review your Asylum Application. Now is the time to make any last additions. It is important that it be accurate. Anything that is misleading or wrong can be used against you by the ICE lawyer.

Next, the judge will enter any evidence into the court record. Whatever documents you submitted will be reviewed. Then the hearing will begin.

You will begin by presenting your story. There is no time limit, so tell your story slowly so the interpreter can properly translate. You should be passionate and emotional. If your experience did not happen to you but happened to a family member, describe the type of person they were and your connection to them. For example: "The gangs have killed my brother and they are going after my entire family. They will go after me in the same way." Then explain why regardless of where you go within your home country, your life will more than likely be in danger. Read *Chapter Four* on developing your story. **Remember, be sincere, passionate, and emotional. Express fear in your face as you recall your experience.** As you speak, provide the examples (exhibits) to help explain your home country's conditions.

Once you have finished your story, the ICE lawyer will tell the judge why you should be deported or will **cross-examine** you. Their job is to convince the judge that the government should deport you. They do that by attempting to find problems with your story. In cross-examination, they may ask you the same question in different ways. You must respond exactly in the same way you presented your story. They will do their best to make you look like you are not telling the truth. Your story cannot change. Again, read *Chapter Four* on developing your story.

You then can present witnesses or experts that will provide additional proof that your story is true. The ICE lawyer and the judge will also have the right to ask them questions.

After the cross-examination is done and the witnesses have spoken, both you and the ICE lawyer will be allowed to make a final statement. Your **closing statement** is very important as it is the last opportunity you will have to convince the judge of your asylum story.

The final decision is up to the judge, who will either make the decision at the end of the hearing or will wait until a later day. If the judge decides later, you will receive the notice in the mail. If the judge approves your case, you will be able to stay in the United States. In the case of asylum, you can apply for a green card one year after the judge has approved your application. If the judge denies your case, you have the right to appeal their decision.

How to Appeal if Your Case is Denied
If the judge decides against you, you still have options, but you need to take action. Unfortunately, some judges will rule against you regardless of how good your story is. You will have 30 days to appeal the judge's decision to the **Board of Immigration Appeals (BIA)**. **Now you MUST use an Immigration Expert to represent you.**

If the judge decides against your case at the end of the hearing, they may say, "Based on the evidence, I am denying your application and am ordering you to be deported to your country of birth." The judge must then say, "Do you want to appeal my decision?" Consult with your lawyer. You will have 30 days to appeal the decision. In the United States, if you do not agree with the decision of one court, you can ask for a higher court to consider your case.

Levels of appeal:
   ✓ **Board of Immigration Appeals (BIA)** – First level
   ✓ **Circuit Court of Appeals** – Second level
   ✓ **Supreme Court** – Third level

If you have a good case and the money to pay for the court costs, you can appeal it all the way to the Supreme Court. The process of appeals can last for many years and may end in your favor.

> **True Story:** In April of 2018, the U.S. Supreme Court decided in favor of the immigrant James Dimaya regarding the definition of a crime-of-violence. The decision now prevents the government from unfairly calling any crime a crime-of-violence. A strong case can help you and possibly even change unfair laws.

If you believe in your story, do not give up.

Part Two: An Interview with an ICE Immigration Officer

The immigration officer's job is to interview you by asking a series of questions in the form of a conversation. They look for problems and inconsistencies with your story. They interview hundreds of people every month and can quickly determine who is telling the truth and who is not.
You will be interviewed by an officer when:
- ✓ You are applying for Affirmative Asylum or UAC
- ✓ You are filing a Marriage Petition or Family Petition
- ✓ You have a consular interview in your home country

In this book, we will cover the most common interviews. If you pass, this may be the last step before you can apply for your green card.

Affirmative Asylum or UAC Interview Process
If you pass your asylum interview, you will receive the Asylee (documented) status. In one year you can apply for a green card.

Marriage or Family Petition Interview
- ✓ Occurs in the U.S. if you are a visa-overstayer

✓ Occurs in your home country if you entered the U.S. without inspection

If you pass your interview, whether inside or outside the United States, Immigration Services will grant you your green card. If you have been married less than two years, you will receive a two-year green card. Before it expires, you will need to submit additional information to prove you are still married and living together. Once that happens, you will receive your ten-year green card. If Immigration Services has more questions, you may be asked to attend another interview.

Be prepared before you go to the interview:
We cannot tell you this enough, **BE PREPARED** and take the interview process seriously.

Asylum/UAC Application: You will describe to the officer how you qualify under one of the **protected grounds.** Your story must be consistent and believable. The interview could last several hours. See *Chapter Four* on developing your story.
✓ **What to bring:** Bring a copy of everything you submitted to Immigration Services plus your identification (ID), passport, and the invitation to the interview.

Marriage Petition: You and your spouse may be interviewed together or separately. The officer will ask you a series of questions. They will look at how you match (age and ability to speak each other's language). They will also look at your body language. Do you look comfortable together? The interview will last 5-30 minutes.
✓ **What to bring:** Bring a copy of everything you submitted to Immigration Services plus identification (IDs) for you and your spouse.

Consular Interview: You will have to return to your birth country and attend an interview in the U.S. Consulate. Often the interview is done through a window, but sometimes it is in a room. The interview could last a few minutes or a whole hour.

✓ **What to bring:** Bring the original documents as well as copies of everything you have submitted to Immigration Services in the past, including a valid passport and two passport photos.

In all cases, dress nicely and arrive early. Be polite to the interviewing officer. They will ask the same question in different ways. If you tell your story consistently, you will have no problems.

It is acceptable to postpone the interview if you have a good reason. Ask in writing or go to the office ahead of time and ask for a new date.

Marriage Petition or Family Petition Interview in the United States

Sample questions the interviewer may ask:
- ✓ How and when did you meet?
- ✓ How long did you date before your spouse proposed?
- ✓ How did your spouse propose to you? Did they give you a ring? What were you doing that moment?
- ✓ Have you met each other's relatives?
- ✓ Are you living together now?
- ✓ What is each other's date of birth?
- ✓ What is the street address where you live?
- ✓ What is the name of your spouse's best friend?
- ✓ Where does your spouse work?
- ✓ What are your favorite things you do on weekends?
- ✓ Does your spouse have a favorite TV show?
- ✓ What about the wedding? How many people were there? Where was it located?
- ✓ Did any of your family members attend the wedding? Who?
- ✓ Have you gone on any vacations? Do you have photos?
- ✓ Are you planning on having any children?
- ✓ Does your spouse have any tattoos on their body?
- ✓ Do you have any documents proving you are living together?
- ✓ Do you both speak the same language?

Marriage Petition or Family Petition Interview in Your Home Country

(Consular Process or Provisional Unlawful Presence Waiver)

ATTENTION: The information below applies only to people who entered the U.S. without inspection (undocumented). You will have to return to your home country for this interview. If you had legal entry (visa overstayer) this does not apply to you.

After you have submitted all of your documents and your Provisional Unlawful Presence Waiver (**I-601A**) is approved, you will receive a notice of appointment in your home country.

You will have to bring:
- ✓ All documents you submitted to the National Visa Center (original version and one set of copies)
- ✓ Medical examination records from authorized physicians
- ✓ Financial documents from the petitioner or another sponsor in your application
- ✓ Signed affidavits (letters) of support
- ✓ Your valid passport
- ✓ Two passport photos

The interview may take only a few minutes. It will be a conversation with an officer who will assess you as a person. Every officer will do the interview differently. Remember to be natural and honest.

Affirmative Asylum Petition or UAC Interview

You will sit across the table from the officer. On the table will be a notepad and the evidence you supplied. The officer will ask a series of questions similar to the ones listed below. As you answer, the officer will be building a mental picture of your story, comparing what you say to the evidence you provided, such as dates, passport stamps, and other documents. For example, if you say you have not visited your home country since arriving here but you have a stamp in your passport proving you did visit, your story will lose credibility. Be prepared for the officer to view your passport, as it is a record of your travels. It should be consistent with your story.

Consider all these potential questions carefully:
- ✓ When did you enter the United States?
- ✓ Did you suffer any physical harm?
- ✓ Do you have any scars to help prove your claim?
- ✓ Is there anyone who can testify to your claims of being harmed or threatened?
- ✓ Have you applied for asylum in any other country? If no, why not?
- ✓ Have you ever committed any terrorist acts?
- ✓ What city were you born in?
- ✓ Are you married, and do you have any children?
- ✓ Have you ever returned to your home country?
- ✓ Were you tortured?
- ✓ Were you ever part of an organization or political party?
- ✓ Have you been harmed?
- ✓ When were you harmed?
- ✓ Have you ever lied on an application form in the United States?
- ✓ Were you ever in prison in your home country? If so, why?

✓ Do you have family members in the United States?
✓ Do you have family members in your home country?
✓ Did the local police in your home country try to stop people from harming you?
✓ Do you fear going back to your home country? If so, why?
✓ Have you lied to anyone about your citizenship while in the United States?
✓ Were you physically harmed in your home country?
✓ Did you try moving to another area in your home country?
✓ After leaving your home country, did you ever return?
✓ Were you forced to commit any crimes?
✓ Do you have any additional evidence or letters you would like to submit?

Notice that several questions sound the same such as "Did you suffer any physical harm?" and "Have you been harmed?" They will ask you the same question differently on purpose. So be aware. Keep your answers short. Do not change your story. Use detail but do not expand your answer beyond the specific question. Again, use emotion when explaining.

Remember, develop your story using *Chapter Four* and practice, practice, practice.

At the end, the officer will ask if you have anything else to add. They will not tell you if you passed or failed your interview. Within two weeks you will return to the office to receive your notice, or you will receive it in the mail. The decision will be one of the following:

✓ **Approval:** The best possible answer. You now have one year to organize your documents and prepare for your green card application.

✓ **Recommended Approval:** You passed the interview, but Immigration Services is waiting for background security checks.
✓ **Deny:** You failed to convince the officer you had
✓ "credible fear." You will have a second chance in immigration court.
✓ **Notice to intend to deny (NOID):** Only occurs if you currently have legal status. The document will state why Immigration Services intends to deny your application. You will have 16 days to respond.

If denied, you will have a second chance to tell your story to an immigration judge. **If you have not hired an Immigration Expert, now is the time.**

Chapter Six

Being Arrested and What ICE Doesn't Want You to Know

"Citizenship to me is more than a piece of paper. Citizenship is also about character. I am an American. We are just waiting for our country to recognize it." –Jose Antonio Vargas

----

What You Will Learn:
- ✓ What to do in an ICE encounter at your house
- ✓ What to do in an ICE or police encounter in public
- ✓ What to do if you are arrested and detained
- ✓ How to stop an expedited deportation
- ✓ How to get released from detention
- ✓ How to navigate detention court and appeals
- ✓ What to do if you are deported

In the United States everyone has rights, including undocumented people. It is important you know your rights.

True Story: It was early, about 7:00 in the morning. Alejandra was walking out of her house on her way to work. Two people approached her and asked if she knew an Antonio and if he lived in the house. She said that he was her husband and he was asleep in the house. They told her that Antonio had called them regarding a crime he had witnessed and that they wanted to speak to him. It was urgent. She said yes and went back into the house. Unfortunately, she did not close the door. Alejandra went into the bedroom and told her husband two people wanted to ask a few questions. He stood up and walked into the living room where suddenly five men were there waiting for him. They were from ICE. Alejandra was legal, but Antonio had no documentation. He had been in the United States since 1980. They were married and had three children. It made no difference. Antonio was arrested and later deported.

What did Alejandra do wrong? She left the door open, and she admitted Antonio was in the house. Knowing he is undocumented, she should have said she didn't know, then she should have closed and locked the door. **Unless ICE had a warrant signed by a judge, they would have had no choice but to leave and try another day.** By then, Alejandra and Antonio could have contacted an Immigration Expert and work out their options.

ICE and the private detention centers see you only as a number. President Trump has promised his supporters he will deport as many undocumented people as he possibly can. ICE will lie, intimidate, and threaten you, or even pretend to be nice to get you to do one thing: to admit you are undocumented so they can arrest and deport you. And if you are in detention, they will make your life even worse. All they want is for you to sign a deportation letter and send you on your way to your birth country. Knowing your rights is important.

An Encounter with ICE at Your Home (Know Your Rights)

If ICE is knocking on your door, do not open it unless they have a search warrant signed by a judge. There are two types of warrants:

Remember

- ✓ **ICE Immigration Warrant:** The top of the document will say "U.S. Department of Justice" and "Warrant for Removal/Deportation." This document gives ICE no power to enter your home or remove any evidence. It only gives ICE the right to detain you if they physically see you.
- ✓ **Judicial Warrant:** The top of the document will say "The United States District Court." The document will have your name and address on the front and will be signed by a judge. This document does give them power to enter your home, arrest you, and take any evidence.

Only a warrant signed by a judge gives ICE the right to come into your house without your permission. DO NOT open the door unless ICE can give you the signed warrant. Tell them to give you the signed warrant through a window or slide it under the door. It MUST have your name and correct address with a signature by a judge. Do not be fooled by ICE.

Be aware that ICE will use tricks to get you to open the door by saying things like:

- ✓ "We are investigating a crime and would like to ask some questions."

✓ "We believe your identity was stolen and would like to ask some questions."
✓ "Can you come out of your house so we can ask some questions about a neighbor?"

They may also use fear by yelling and threatening to break the door down. Tell ICE you cannot help them and they need to leave. They will lie to you and say anything to get you to open the door. If you open the door and they ask if they can come in, say no. Again, unless they have a valid warrant, they cannot arrest you in your home. They will have no choice but to leave. If ICE pushes their way into your house with force, they are violating your rights. You have every right to record it on your phone. They have no right to take your phone or any documents. If they violate your rights, have proof such as a cellphone video recording and call an Immigration Expert.

An Encounter with Police or ICE in Public
In the United States, no one except ICE can investigate and arrest undocumented people. The local police only have the power to arrest you if there is a warrant for you. **However, if you are out in public and have not committed any crimes, neither ICE nor the police have the power to randomly ask your immigration status.**

Some states, including **Arizona, Alabama, Georgia, and Texas,** have passed laws allowing the local police to ask about your citizenship but only if you are doing something else that is in violation of the law, such as speeding or driving with a broken taillight. Police can only ask you for a government ID such as a passport or driver license. They cannot ask you about your citizenship or birth country. If you are walking around in public, you do not have to carry any ID. If they ask, say: **"I am sorry, I do not have any ID on me. Am I doing anything wrong? Can you tell me what law I am breaking?"**

If the officer ignores your questions, ask again. However, do not lie to the officer and do be polite. Do not say you are a United States citizen unless you are.

If You Are Arrested by ICE Agents
Remember your rights and always cooperate with ICE, but do not give them any unnecessary information. Ask for the reason they are arresting you.

Know your rights:
- ✓ You have the right to remain silent
- ✓ You have the right to speak to your lawyer before you speak to Immigration Services
- ✓ Except for giving them your name, remain silent until you have your lawyer present
- ✓ Do not admit anything such as where you are from
- ✓ Do not sign anything until your lawyer is present

You want to say in English or Spanish:

"Please know I have chosen to exercise my right to remain silent and to refuse to answer your questions. If you detain me, I request to contact my lawyer immediately. I am also exercising my right not to sign anything until I speak with my lawyer."

No matter how hard the officer may try, do not sign anything (except for signing your fingerprint card). Do not give them your home address, and do not say you are undocumented. However, do not lie to them because any lies will be used against you in court. It is okay to be silent but not to lie. **Remember, be polite and be cooperative. However, do not sign any paper that forces you to admit guilt.**

Always carry documentation with you that proves you have

been in the United States for more than two years. President Trump changed the rules in February 2017 so if you cannot prove you have been in the United States at least two years, you could end up in expedited deportation (no court hearing). Proof can be a check stub, utility bill, or receipt with the date and your name on it. If you have filed for any status (asylum, Marriage Petition, and so on) keep a copy of the receipt notice with you always.

What Not to Carry:

Remember

- ✓ Do not carry fake identification or documents such as a fake social security card
- ✓ Do not carry your home country passport
- ✓ Do not carry any papers from your home country
- ✓ Do not carry any documents with your home address
- ✓ If your phone contains information such as home addresses, keep it password protected

ICE will use whatever you have on you to find other undocumented friends and family. When arrested, if you leave any personal belongings behind such as a car, only ask documented people to collect your property. Tell undocumented family and friends to stay away. ICE may use your car or belongings as bait to capture them as well. You should leave an extra set of keys at home so that someone can move the vehicle to a safe place.

As we have stated several times in this book, you must have an Immigration Expert available to assist with your questions. If you are arrested and detained, call your lawyer and then call your family. **Everything will be taken from you, so memorize the telephone numbers for your family and Immigration Expert. Also, memorize your A-Number if you have one.** If you do not have an A-Number, they will issue you one. Your family and friends should also know your A-Number. They can call the court case hotline, **1-800-898-7180** and enter the A-Number to receive up-to-date information about your case. The call is an automated service, and it will not track the caller's location.

During processing, they will take your fingerprints and photos. Later, the officers will begin to pressure you. They will ask you to admit you have been in the United States without documentation. They will make your life as difficult as possible. They will tell you that you could be there for months or years if you refuse to sign a deportation order. If you sign it, you agree not to see a judge, and you are on your way to your home country.

If you have a good story explaining why you are here, and it is NOT only about seeking a better life, you should ask for asylum for fear of being returned to your country. Then tell them you must speak to your Immigration Expert BEFORE any interviews. If you do not have an Immigration Expert, they must give you a list of lawyers you can call. However, picking a random lawyer from a list means you are taking a chance. Read *Chapter Five* and *Chapter Seven* on what happens in the court process and how to pick a lawyer.

The process for fighting your deportation could take months, and you may be in detention the entire time. If you have a good argument and your Immigration Expert agrees, DO NOT GIVE UP. This will be your chance to stop your deportation.

Be aware of fraudulent lawyers. Unfortunately, some unethical lawyers take advantage of people in detention. They will take your money knowing you have little or no chance of success. When you hire an Immigration Expert, do your homework and ask for references you can call to ask about the quality of their services. Read *Chapter Seven* on finding an Immigration Expert. It is best to find an Immigration Expert BEFORE you are arrested.

When detained by police or ICE, ICE has 48 hours to initiate deportation proceedings, or they must release you. Sometimes ICE may detain you for longer periods by placing a "hold" to give ICE more time to build their case. **In no way can ICE or the police hold you for more than 72 hours without ICE giving you a Notice to Appear (NTA).** An Immigration Expert can use any violations of your rights against ICE by filing a **motion to suppress.** Furthermore, according to the United States Constitution, ICE cannot use evidence obtained without a proper warrant against you. This includes physical evidence, such as documents, and witness statements. Once illegally-obtained evidence is excluded, ICE may not have enough proof against you in removal hearings.

Here is a tip: If it is the police you are dealing with and not ICE, if you convince the officer you have been in the United States several years and you have young children at home, they may feel for you and let you go. It is up to the officer.

Possible Ways to Be Released from Detention

These days, it is more difficult to be released from detention with Trump in office. However, if an immigration judge has determined you have a reasonable case, you will either remain in detention until your final hearing or be released on **bond.**

Bond: A bond is a set amount paid to the government in return for your release. It works as a guarantee that you will attend all court hearings. If you attend all the hearings and agree to whatever happens to you, the government will return the money.

The judge or the immigration officers will set the bond. The detained person will receive a paper stating: "Notice of Custody Determination." On it is an amount requested for the bond. Your Immigration Expert should be present at any hearings to help minimize the bond amount. Not everyone is eligible for a bond. It depends on your charges and risk of not returning to court if released. The detention center generally has a list of local bondsmen that can assist you with this. A lawyer can help you arrange a bondsman.

Order of Supervision: Whether you already have an Order of Removal or you are still waiting for a court hearing, there may be certain special circumstances (such as illness or family care-taking) which your Immigration Expert can use to request that you be released under an Order of Supervision. This allows you to organize your life and belongings before deportation. As part of the agreement, you will have to report to ICE on a regular basis and possibly wear an ankle bracelet.

Because President Trump is not hiring enough judges, the court hearing can take anywhere from months to years. You should work with your Immigration Expert to find a reason why you should be released. If you are successful, you will be required to report to ICE on a regular basis.

What You Need to Remember if You Are Deported

If deported under force, you will only be allowed to return to your home country with one suitcase and up to 40 pounds of clothing. Immigration Services will take away any U.S. identification. Depending on your circumstances, Immigration

Services may release you with an ankle bracelet, so you can organize your personal belongings. If you are not released, you must ask for your belongings to be organized through someone you trust.

If you are deported:

✓ **Have a bank card that works in your home country**. Your trusted friends or family back in the United States can sell off your assets and deposit the money into your account. You can have immediate access to money at an ATM in your country.

✓ **Collect any unpaid wages you earned.** Contact your former employer and inform them that you will have a friend pick up your final check. Your employer is required to pay you for any work you did even if you were undocumented.

✓ **You are entitled to tax refunds.** If you have been paying taxes in the United States, you are entitled to tax refunds even if you are undocumented. Ask a trusted friend to work with a tax preparer and have them submit your taxes. You can even have the money sent to your address in your home country.

✓ **Do not carry anything of value.** Thieves in your home country assume you are returning with money or items of value. Ship anything of value via a service like Federal Express to your address in your home country.

✓ **Have an address set up in your home country prior to your deportation.** If you know you will be deported, it's smart to have a phone and money sent to your new address ahead of time.

Warning: There are thieves waiting for unsuspecting deportees in your home country. In a common scam, they will allow you to borrow their phone when you arrive, so you can call your relatives. Then later, the thieves will use the phone numbers you entered to call your relatives, tell them you are being held hostage, and demand money for your release.

Finally, if you are deported (whether voluntarily or by force) you could be barred from re-entry for three years to life. However, if you still believe you have a right to live in the United States, you have options for legally returning. For example, perhaps you had a bad lawyer who did not represent you well. In this case, you will need the help of a new lawyer or Immigration Expert. Our suggestion is to consult with one to understand your options.

STEP FOUR:
Read *Chapter Seven* and carefully select an Immigration Expert who you can trust and help you through the process.

<u>Chapter Seven</u>

Finding an Immigration Expert You Can Trust

"People come here penniless but not cultureless. They bring us gifts. We can synthesize the best of our traditions with the best of theirs. We can teach and learn from each other to produce a better America..."
–Mary Pipher

What You Will Learn:
- ✓ Legal representation
  - o Lawyers
  - o Authorized Immigration Providers
  - o Non-profit legal assistance organizations
  - o Notary and everyone else
- ✓ Selecting your Immigration Expert
- ✓ Fees and payments
- ✓ Working with an Immigration Expert
- ✓ Dealing with a bad lawyer
- ✓ Communicating with your Immigration Expert

Words to Know:

Immigration Expert: a lawyer or person authorized by a state or federal government agency to provide immigration services. We do NOT suggest notaries or others who are not authorized by a state or federal government.

Introduction

In all our conversations with undocumented immigrants, there are three common reasons why they have not attempted to become documented:

- ✓ They do not understand the legal system
- ✓ They do not believe they have any options for becoming legal
- ✓ They fear lawyers will rip them off

Unfortunately, there are many bad lawyers and notaries that only want your money. However, there are good lawyers dedicated to helping immigrants like you. We will help you find an Immigration Expert who you can trust. Because immigration law is continuously changing, finding the right Immigration Expert who does the research and finds the best path for you is important. Getting through the immigration process can be difficult and expensive, but it is worth it.

The Immigration Expert: To our knowledge, only in immigration law can a qualified non-lawyer represent a client in court and provide advice. Throughout this book, we use the term "Immigration Expert" to mean a practicing lawyer, law student, law graduate, reputable individual, accredited representative, or accredited individual. These are people with extensive experience in immigration law.

Be careful; Immigration Experts are not all the same:
Becoming documented is much more than filling out the right forms and paying money. A good Immigration Expert has years of experience. Do not pick a person just because of the price.

Lawyers

Lawyers go to school for around eight years before they graduate with a degree. Then they must pass the state exam before they begin practicing law. Lawyers practice many types of law. A lawyer who is good at criminal defense law may not be good at immigration law. It is important to do your research and pick the right one. **Be aware that there are good lawyers and there are others who only want your money**. For example, in 2015, an immigration lawyer in Boulder, Colorado went to prison for six years for scamming immigrant families out of tens of thousands of dollars.

Also, if your case includes any criminal convictions, you want to find a lawyer who has experience with both immigration law and criminal law.

Authorized Immigration Providers

The U.S. Department of Justice's Executive Office for Immigration Review created the Authorized Provider of Immigration Services program. The program allows people who are not lawyers to provide legal advice, help you fill out forms, and even represent you in court. They can do everything a lawyer can within immigration law. An Authorized Provider must have a minimum of two years of experience working in immigration and be approved by the U.S. Government on their knowledge of the law. Authorized Providers work either with a lawyer or in a non-profit organization. They cannot operate a business on their own. Again, like lawyers, there are also good and bad Authorized Providers. Check the resources listed in the *Useful Websites and Phone Numbers* part of this book to find accredited organizations and individuals.

Non-Profit Immigration Assistance Organizations

Across the United States are non-profit organizations that can help you with immigration matters. You can find them through your church, through the internet, or by speaking to friends. One of the largest is the **Catholic Legal Immigration Network**. Non-profit legal assistance organizations use lawyers who are willing to contribute their time for free. They can help you in several ways, such as answering your questions, helping you fill out forms, teaching you English, and more. They can only represent you if your income is below a certain level. Most do not handle detention cases as they take so much time, but they generally know the good lawyers from the bad ones and can assist you in finding a lawyer. We provide a link in the *Useful Websites and Phone Numbers* part of this book that can help you find the non-profit immigration organization closest to you.

Notaries and Other Immigration Assistants

Although a notary can assist you in some legal matters, they cannot help you with your immigration papers. A notary is a person with the legal right to assist you with minor legal needs, but **it is illegal for them to provide you with any advice.** Also, **they cannot represent you in court**. There are honest notaries, but unfortunately many more dishonest ones. In addition to notaries, some people call themselves "Immigration Consultants," "Document Consultants," and "Immigration Specialists." These could be scams and you should do your research before giving your money to one.

How to Hire an Immigration Expert

Take your time and meet with more than one Immigration Expert before choosing who to work with. The best way to find someone is through:
- ✓ Friends and family members who have been successful with their case
- ✓ Your church minister
- ✓ A non-profit immigration office

If possible, make a list of three or four Immigration Experts recommended by people you know. Then set up meetings. These consultations will cost $0-$150. You should know if there is a consultation fee at the time you set up the meeting. Don't be attracted to someone only because they have no consultation fee. These consultations can be valuable as they can help you determine your chances of success.

In the first consultation, ask them:
- ✓ How many years they have been practicing immigration law
- ✓ How many immigration cases they have handled
- ✓ How many cases like yours have they handled
- ✓ If they have experience with criminal law (only if you have criminal convictions)
- ✓ What they think your chances of becoming documented are, based on each of the possible ways listed in this book

A good Immigration Expert has been practicing immigration law for more than two years and has closed over 100 cases. Also, ask if they handle detention cases. If detained, you want to know they are there for you. Give them the details of your case and ask what experience they have in similar cases.

Ask what they think your chances are. Do not trust a lawyer or representative who says there is a "100% chance" that you will receive a green card. Saying "100%" is unrealistic and could be a sign of a bad lawyer. If both you and the Immigration Expert are comfortable with the relationship, you will sign an agreement of representation.

Fees and Payments
Most lawyers charge by the hour. A typical Immigration Expert will charge a flat fee based on the services and then by the hour for special projects.

After understanding your case at the initial consultation meeting, the Immigration Expert should be able to give you an idea of what they can do for you and what your case will cost, assuming you have provided all details of your past. Keep in mind that sometimes they learn something new about your case along the way that may have an impact on the cost.

As for payment, every Immigration Expert is different:
- ✓ Some will require all cash up front
- ✓ Some will require a percentage down and the balance before sending in your application
- ✓ Some will allow installment payments with a down payment

Your Money

When you make payments to the lawyer, many states require your money to be deposited into a special trust account under your name for safety. Your Immigration Expert cannot touch it unless they have completed the work and sent an invoice to the trust.

But not all states require trust accounts. For example, Arizona has no requirement in most cases. Colorado, on the other hand, requires all money to be deposited into the trust account. The contract with your Immigration Expert should state how they keep your money.

While working with your Immigration Expert and making payments, **you should require a monthly statement of the work they did and how your money was applied.** If for some reason you decide to change lawyers, or you decide to not go through with your application, you can request any unused money and a copy of all documents relating to your case. Unless your contract with the Immigration Expert specifically states otherwise, you are in your right to **ask for any unused**

portions of your money back. They are required to provide you with all documents relating to your case. They should only charge you a small fee to copy the documents.

Communicating with Your Immigration Expert

You will have several meetings with your Immigration Expert. Depending on the complexity of your case, the relationship can last for years. The immigration process is slow, so it is important to be patient. When your Immigration Expert asks for documents, bring them as quickly as possible. Remember to attend every appointment.

When working with your Immigration Expert, be sure to:

- ✓ Contact their office at least once a month to check on your case
- ✓ Let them know if you change your address or phone number
- ✓ Provide them with documents for your case as quickly as possible when they ask
- ✓ Be on time for every appointment with them
- ✓ Attend your court hearings with them
- ✓ Ask them (or their assistant) what the next steps are after each meeting
- ✓ Make your payments on time
- ✓ Ask for copies of all the documents they file to Immigration Services

It is a good idea to keep a planner or notebook with you each time you meet with your Immigration Expert. Write down what was said at the meeting and the names of everyone you speak with at the office.

Be Prepared with Documents

The United States court system in part relies on evidence to support your case. Evidence includes documents that support who you are, where you came from, proof of what happened to you in your home country (for asylum), and your status.

You may be asked for:
- ✓ Your birth certificate
- ✓ Children's birth certificates
- ✓ Marriage certificate
- ✓ Your former address in your home country
- ✓ Job information (who you worked for, how long, and where in the U.S.)
- ✓ IDs such as passport and driver license
- ✓ Income taxes if you have paid them in the U.S.
- ✓ Copies of police records if you were ever arrested
- ✓ Copies of any letters from Immigration Services
- ✓ Photos or news articles regarding your experience in your home country (for asylum)

Listen to your Immigration Expert carefully. Know that some documents may need to be translated into English and certified. Be honest with them about your history. For example, tell them if you were married and divorced in your home country, were ever arrested, or have criminal charges. Tell them every detail so they can prepare properly and not be surprised by something the court finds out about you. If you do that, the process will go smoothly.

Dealing with a Bad Lawyer

You are paying the lawyer for a service. If they fail to perform that service by missing a court date or not mailing your application on time, which results in a problem with your case, you can complain and make them correct the problem. No lawyer can guarantee success, but they should guarantee the quality of their work. Study your monthly statement and ask questions about what they have done since last month. You should know there will be many months where nothing happens as they are waiting for a response from Immigration Services. **A lawyer should not charge you twice for the same**

service. If they are charging you more than the original estimate, ask them to explain.

Give your lawyer the opportunity to fix any errors. If they ignore your calls, fail to make good on their work, or require you to pay money for a consultation regarding your bill, tell them you may have to file a complaint (grievance) against them.

Lawyers do not want a complaint against their name. It will appear on their records and could result in them losing their license. There are two ways you can file a claim against a bad lawyer. The first way requires the use of the internet. Every state has a State Bar Association. The State Bar Association has the power to determine if your complaint is valid, and if so, to force the bad lawyer to give you your money back. If you feel your lawyer has not treated you fairly, call the main office in Washington DC and ask for the State Bar Association closest to you. The address is:

Commission on Immigration
American Bar Association
1050 Connecticut Avenue, NW
Suite 400
Washington, DC 20036

Phone: 202-662-1005
Email: **immcenter@americanbar.org**
Website: **www.americanbar.org/immigration**

Once you have a new Immigration Expert, tell them your experience with your old lawyer. If they agree to help you, they can also file the complaint about the old lawyer on your behalf. You may even get some money back.

Points to Remember When Hiring an Immigration Expert:
- ✓ Do not hire anyone who refuses to give you a written contract
- ✓ Do not trust anyone who "100% guarantees" that you will get a green card
- ✓ Do not trust anyone who asks you to lie on a form

Once You Hire Your Immigration Expert:
- ✓ Ask for a monthly statement of what work they have done
- ✓ Tell them if your home address or phone number changes
- ✓ Provide documents as fast as possible when they ask

<u>Chapter Eight</u>

Making a Backup Plan and Being Prepared

"Your enemy is not the refugee. Your enemy is the one that made him a refugee." –Tariq Ramadan

----

What You Will Learn:
- ✓ Being organized and keeping all your papers in one place
- ✓ Making sure you have an Immigration Expert available
- ✓ Creating a Power of Attorney
- ✓ Establishing a bank account for emergencies
- ✓ Setting family meetings to be prepared

Introduction

One of the most painful experiences you might encounter is arriving home to find out a family member has been detained at a raid and is on their way to deportation. We hope it will not happen to you, but if it does, the best way to deal with this is to have a plan. This chapter will help you know what to do now and how to be prepared should anything happen to you or a family member.

> If a family has not made preparations and both parents are detained by ICE, it's possible that their children will end up in state custody and will be turned over to foster parents. It can be very difficult to get them back.

Organize your life so you are best prepared for whatever happens.

A problem we often hear is that people don't keep important papers. Becoming documented requires that you provide papers to prove your past.

1) **Keep all your papers in one place**. A common problem we hear is that people don't keep their important papers organized. Your first step is to purchase a closeable box, briefcase, or anything you can use to secure your documents in one place. You will keep all your personal, legal, and financial documents in the box. You will need these papers to become documented. Be sure to keep your box in a safe place. Unless they have a warrant signed by a judge, ICE has no authority to touch any personal items including your papers.

Your box should include:

a. A list of names and phone numbers of family and friends to contact if something happens. That includes the name and contact information for your Immigration Expert

b. A list of everyone's "**A-Numbers**," if relevant

c. Original and copies of everyone's birth certificates

d. Everyone's passports (you should never carry them on you)

e. Your children's Social Security cards if they have them

f. Receipts or papers with your name and dates to prove how long you have been living in the United States

g. Pay stubs from all current and past jobs along with the names of companies you have worked for while here in the United States

h. Copies of any current and past home lease agreements and former addresses where you have lived

i. All identification cards (IDs) except what you need to carry daily such as driver license and auto insurance cards

j. If you are working with an Immigration Expert, copies of all documents sent to the immigration office and letters mailed to you by Immigration Services

k. If you pay taxes, copies of any tax returns, even if you used a fake Social Security number or **Individual Taxpayer Identification Number (ITIN)**

We have found that few people keep their records. This is a big mistake. It's important to keep all papers, IDs, and documents on this list for your immigration expert to help build a case.

You do not need to keep everyday receipts such as receipts from the grocery store. A safe rule would be to keep everything with your name on it.

2) **Have an Immigration Expert available.** Another mistake is not having an Immigration Expert when you need one. If detained, it is important that you have someone to call who you know. It is difficult to find one when you are in detention. Even if you cannot become documented now, you should still have one or two Immigration Experts you can call. Remember, you cannot use a notary for this as they cannot represent you in court. Make sure that the Immigration Expert handles detention cases. You also want to memorize their phone number in case you get detained.

3) **Create a Power of Attorney.** If you are detained, a Power of Attorney is a paper that gives temporary custody of your children and assets to a trusted person. Without a Power of Attorney, any U.S.-born children of parents who are deported could be taken by the government and placed in a foster home with strangers. Moreover, you could lose any assets you own such as vehicles, your house, and other property.

There are two kinds of Power of Attorney agreements:
✓ A "**general**" agreement covers everything you own and custody of your children
✓ A "**separate**" Power of Attorney is where one person takes care of your belongings while another person takes custody of your children

The person you choose for Power of Attorney must either have a green card or be a U.S. citizen. They can be a relative or a friend you trust to take care of your personal belongings if you are detained or deported. Your Immigration Expert or a notary can help you complete the agreement, which will include the following information:

✓ **Children:** List their complete names, dates of birth, and Social Security numbers.
✓ **Personal belongings:** List bank account numbers, vehicles with Vehicle Identification Numbers (VIN), address of the house, and location of your assets.

True Story: Federal immigration agents picked up a Luis, a young mother who was living undocumented in the United States. She was detained for about a month, separated from her 7-year-old son Daniel and infant daughter Angie, who were both born in the United States. She was taken to the airport to be deported. She expected to meet her children there for the flight to Guatemala, but they were not there. "There was no Angie, no Daniel," she recalls. The officer told her, "Your children are going to stay in the United States with the state. Your children aren't going to Guatemala." Boarding the plane that would take her thousands of miles away from them, Luis said, "I wanted to kill myself. I wanted to die."

A **Power of Attorney** giving temporary child custody to someone Luis trusts would have stopped this.

NOTE: A Power of Attorney is only good for the state you created it in. If you moved from Texas to Colorado, for example, you would have to create a new agreement in Colorado.

4) **Establish a bank account with emergency funds.** If deported, you will have little or no money to take to your home country. And if you do take money, it is not uncommon to be robbed when you arrive. It's a good idea to keep a little money in a bank account that you

can withdraw from wherever you are. Friends in the United States can also deposit money which you can withdraw in your home country at any ATM. It's much easier than a Western Union wire if you have a bank card.

5) **Plan to have someone contact the detained person's work.** If the detained person will be released in a few days, let their employer know so that they can hold their position for them. If they will not be released, ask their employer for their final paycheck. Have a plan for who will do this for you if you ever get detained.

6) **Set up a meeting with family and trusted friends**. Once a year or so, the family should discuss all the points found in the first section of this book. Everyone should know the location of the family box, the contact information for your Immigration Expert, and how to access money.

7) **Set up an address in your home country.** Know that there are thieves waiting for you in your home country. To protect yourself, have your family mail a phone, money, and personal items to an address that you trust in your home country via a courier such as Federal Express so it is there when you arrive.

Only documented people should visit detained people. If you are undocumented or unsure of your legal status in the U.S., do not go. ICE may detain you if you go and lie about your legal status. The best option is to call your Immigration Expert and work on getting that person released.

Points to Remember:

✓ Purchase a file box and keep all papers in it.

- ✓ Develop a list of contacts to call if something happens.
- ✓ Find at least one Immigration Expert you can call on.
- ✓ Create a Power of Attorney for custody of your children and assets.
- ✓ Contact the detained person's work and ask for their last paycheck if necessary.
- ✓ Hold regular family meetings so everyone is prepared.
- ✓ Memorize your A-Number (if you have one).
- ✓ Memorize your Immigration Expert's phone number.
- ✓ Memorize the phone number of someone who can help you if you are detained.

Chapter Nine

How to Avoid Being Detained by ICE

"I've always argued that this country has benefited immensely from the fact that we draw people from all over the world." –Alan Greenspan

----

What You Will Learn:
- ✓ How to drive in public without being noticed
- ✓ How to walk in public and avoid ICE
- ✓ What to know when using public transportation
- ✓ How to avoid being a victim of an ICE raid
- ✓ What to know about the people around you
- ✓ What you should not put on social media
- ✓ How ICE tries to locate you
- ✓ What tricks ICE may use to arrest you

Words to Know:

ICE: Immigration and Customs Enforcement. Part of the Homeland Security of the U.S. Government. Their job in part is to investigate and arrest known undocumented people living in the U.S.

CBP: Customs and Border Protection. Part of the Homeland Security of the U.S. Government. Their job, along with Border Patrol, is to prevent undocumented people, smugglers, and others from entering the United States.

True Story: In Georgia, Diaz Lopez was driving himself and another man to a plumbing project when he saw the lights of a police car flashing behind him. He pulled over. The police officer came up to Diaz's window and said he pulled the car over because the man in the passenger's seat was not wearing his seatbelt. The police officer asked for Diaz's driver license, but Diaz did not have one. In most U.S. states, such as Georgia, a person can be arrested and taken to jail for driving without a license. Diaz was arrested and found to be undocumented. A few hours later, ICE came by the police station and took Diaz to the detention center for possible deportation. Though Diaz had lived in America for eleven years, a seatbelt violation may have sent him back to his home country.

Introduction

This chapter helps you minimize your chances of ICE catching and detaining you. We will explain many of the tricks that ICE plays.

Driving in Public without Being Noticed

In the United States, every driver must have a valid driver license, and every car must have up-to-date registration tags and proof of automotive insurance.

When you drive, don't give the police a reason to pull you over. While it is illegal for police to pull you over because of the color of your skin, it is legal to pull you over because of a cracked windshield or a passenger not wearing a seatbelt. If you don't have a valid driver license, they can impound your car and arrest you.

ICE is using a new device called license plate recognition. It can automatically "see" the license plate and identify the owner of the car.

If ICE agents know you are here and they have a deportation order, it's not uncommon for them to follow you while they look for an opportunity to arrest you. Be aware of who is behind you when driving. If a vehicle takes the same turns as you do, drive to a safe zone such as a church or school and wait for them to leave. After that, call your Immigration Expert right away.

Here are some tips when driving:
- ✓ Keep your vehicle as close to its original condition as possible. Making customized changes to its paint jobs, rims, and so on could attract police attention.
- ✓ Keep your license, registration, and insurance up to date. Don't give the police any reason to ask any additional questions if you are pulled over.
- ✓ Every few days, check your car for anything that the police might use to pull you over. Examples include cracked windshields, broken headlights or taillights, and expired license plate tags.
- ✓ If you live within **100 miles** of the border, be aware of random and permanent border patrol checks.
- ✓ Follow the local driving laws in detail. If you don't know the rules, find the local Department of Motor Vehicle office. Most likely they will have an instruction book in your language for free.
- ✓ If you get a parking ticket or a driving ticket, pay it as soon as possible.
- ✓ Do not carry any fake documents with you. Do not give the police a fake document and do not lie to them about being a United States citizen.

You also may consider tinting your windows. While it is against the law to be pulled over because of the color of your skin, some police still do that.

It's more common in areas where police have an agreement with ICE. Tinted windows will reduce your chances of being noticed.

If you are ever in a vehicle accident where no one is injured, try to work it out with the other person and no police. However, if an injury is involved, every state requires you to report it to the police. If someone calls the police, remain calm, do not cause suspicion, and have all your documents in order. Be aware of state laws; while many states do not require you to report an accident, many others do. Also, do not drive away from an accident. If you are caught driving away, the charges are serious, and this will almost guarantee your deportation.

Walking in Public and Avoiding ICE
Walking around in public is safe if you don't bring attention to yourself. Be sure to obey all laws and not do anything that draws attention. Be aware of who is around you. Unless you need your IDs, leave them at home. **No law requires you to carry an ID when walking around in public.**

It's against the law for someone to ask about your immigration status. If the police approach you and ask your status, ignore the question and ask if you are breaking any laws. If they keep asking, repeat your question but don't answer their question. You do not have to answer the question about your citizenship status unless you are at a border or in front of a judge. Eventually, they will have to give up. If they arrest you for some reason, do not say anything to them except that you would like to speak to your lawyer. However, be sure to physically cooperate and not resist.

Here are some tips when walking around:
- ✓ Follow all laws, such as crossing the street in a crosswalk.
- ✓ Don't do anything that draws attention to you.
- ✓ Don't carry any forms of identification with you unless you are doing something that requires it.
- ✓ Stay in public areas such as around shops and businesses. In some neighborhoods, walking around may cause suspicion and result in someone calling the police.

Using Public Transportation
Again, anytime you are in public you are taking a risk. There are many forms of public transportation in the United States. **You are generally safe to travel on public transportation if you have a valid ID and you are not within 100 miles of any U.S. Border.**

- ✓ **City buses, subways, and taxis:** There are no known reports of ICE searching city buses, subways, or taxis, but regardless, use caution—especially if you are close to the U.S. border. You do not need an ID to ride these, so remain silent and refuse to answer if anyone asks.

- ✓ **Airlines:** If you are **flying** somewhere in the United States and you have a valid ID such as a passport from your home country or a U.S. driver license, they will not ask you about your immigration status for domestic flights. We know of no database between the airlines and ICE. At the airport, the Transportation Security Administration (TSA) inspectors will ask for a valid government ID such as a current driver license or passport, but this is only to compare it with the name on the ticket. You cannot fly outside the country while undocumented or in proceedings. If in proceedings, you must file an Application for Travel Document (**I-131**) before travel abroad. However, President Trump has eliminated the possibility of international travel for DACA recipients. Also, to be safe, your flight should not begin or end within **100 miles** of the border.

✓ **Greyhound buses and trains:** Taking a Greyhound bus or a train is risky if you are within 100 miles of the U.S. Border. If you are within 100 miles, there is a good chance border patrol will board the Greyhound bus or the train and ask for papers. The internet has numerous videos of border patrol officers on Greyhound buses and trains asking people about their citizenship. Traveling around the United States on train or bus is safer if you are more than 100 miles from the border. Before you take a trip on the train or bus, check to make sure.

ICE Raids at Work

With Former President Obama, the policy was for ICE to ignore workplaces and focus on criminals. Now, President Trump is going after everyone, including employers who hire undocumented people. For example, in January 2018, ICE raided over 100 convenience stores in a single day across the country. While at work, you should be aware of all the exits and ways you can leave if ICE comes through the door. When ICE conducts a raid, it's because they have reason to believe the employer hires undocumented people, or because a person they are looking for works at the same place as you. ICE does not conduct random raids on businesses. If you have a choice, work at places with the fewest undocumented people to reduce the chances of ICE raids.

Here are some tips for when you are at work:

- ✓ Do not carry any IDs, especially fake ones.
- ✓ If you are in legal proceedings and you have any letters from **USCIS** to prove it, in this situation you **should** keep a valid ID and a copy of the letter with you.
- ✓ In the event of an ICE raid, be aware of all possible ways out of the building.
- ✓ If you are arrested in a raid, do not say, sign, or admit anything. Only ask to call your Immigration Expert. Remember to physically cooperate with the ICE agents.

ICE Raids at Home

ICE often conducts early morning raids on homes when people are leaving for work. Again, these are not random. They only target homes if they have confidence that the person they are looking for lives there. If no one in your home has an immigration warrant, it's unlikely they will target your house. Always be aware of what is around you. Get to know your neighborhood and which cars belong to others who live in the area. ICE often uses two or three unmarked SUVs with dark tinted windows, and most ICE raids include four to six officers.

If you are approached by ANY stranger asking about people in your house, do not give them any information. You can say, "Let me check." When you go back into the house, <u>do not let them in.</u> Go inside and lock the door behind you. Unless they have a real warrant signed by a judge, they have no right to enter your house unless you give permission. While at home, keep your doors locked. Unless ICE has a warrant signed by a judge, they have no right to enter your house. However, they will if you leave the door open. They may even put their foot in the door to try to keep it open. Tell them you do not permit them to enter the house and to remove their foot. In time, they will leave.

Here are some tips for when you are at home:

Remember

- ✓ Remember to keep your doors locked.
- ✓ Do not open the door unless you know who is on the other side.
- ✓ Consider installing a peephole in the door so you know who is on the other side.
- ✓ Consider installing door chains so if you open the door, ICE agents cannot push their way in.
- ✓ If a stranger knocks on your door and asks you for information about someone you know, tell them you don't know anything about the people in the neighborhood. Then close and lock the door.

There have been reports of ICE agents breaking down people's doors. Unless they have a valid warrant signed by a judge, this is illegal. Use your phone and start recording the incident. They cannot touch anything in the house including your phone. Your home should be a safe place, and it can be if you follow our suggestions and stay aware of what is around you.

True Story: In New York, an undocumented high school girl was walking across the school parking lot, and the moment she reached an area where no one could see her, ICE came out of their cars and arrested her. Her charge: association with gang members of MS-13. The evidence: someone observed her at school sitting with confirmed MS-13 members. School officials also found a small amount of marijuana in her locker. The judge in the case dropped the charges, but only after she spent a month in detention.

Know the People around You

Another young student was suspended from school and detained because he wrote the numbers 503 (the country code for El Salvador) in a notebook.

It is not illegal to be a member of a gang. However, in Trump's America, this is a possible ticket to deportation regardless of your legal status. If ICE has connected you to a gang, it is a major count against your ability to become documented. Even a photograph of you walking out of a suspected gang member's house can get you deported. Do not allow someone to post your photo with any associated gang members to Facebook, Instagram, Twitter, or other social media sites.

Friends and Family: It's not only gangs you should be concerned about. Friends and family can also create unexpected threats. However, you can learn to manage the risks. You need to be aware of anyone possibly associated with a crime or even a missed court date. According to ICE, there are 540,000 deportation orders outstanding.

There is a term ICE uses called **"collateral Arrests:** Collateral arrests are people who end up being arrested even though they were not the original target. Approximately 40% of undocumented people arrested in 2017 were collateral arrests according to Homeland Security data. This occurs when ICE enters a home or business to arrest your friend, relative, or coworker because of a warrant, and you happen to be there. Because you are there, ICE will ask you for your papers as well. If you cannot prove you are legally in the United States, you too are arrested. You should only visit or stay with friends who do not have a warrant.

How do you know if ICE is looking for you, a friend, or a family member? If someone was EVER detained and released, they have an **A-Number**. If they ignored court hearings or appointments, chances are they have a deportation order and ICE is looking for them. To know for sure, call: 1-800-898-7180 and enter their A-number. Don't worry, they cannot trace the call to your location.

Social Media

In a recent hearing, a U.S. Senator stated that ICE is investing in advanced research for ALL forms of social media. They intend to use this to investigate and track down undocumented people. This technology can be used to even find your location when you use a computer. You should be extremely careful of what you post on online.

Be careful what you post on any social media website:
- ✓ Don't have pictures of you associated with a gang
- ✓ Don't post pictures of you making gang symbols even as a joke
- ✓ Don't post any pictures of your friends making gang symbols
- ✓ Don't post anything that might be illegal and have a negative impact on your application
- ✓ Don't write about anything that might cause a problem with your immigration paperwork
- ✓ If you are undocumented and a deportation order has been issued for you, delete your account or at least change your name so it cannot be searched for

> **True Story:** It was June of 2017, and Jose, a DACA recipient, was working with his lawyer to obtain his change of status through a Family Petition. About halfway through the process, he received a notice that Immigration Services had suspended his application. The reason? During the background check, immigration officers conducted a routine review of his Facebook page and found some photographs that Jose posted of a party he attended. The photographs included some random people he didn't know. Unfortunately, two of the people were confirmed gang members. This one post could cause him to lose his chance of becoming documented. In Trump's government, guilt by association is enough to get you into trouble.

ICE: How They Find You

As we mentioned earlier, ICE rarely conducts random raids. They use a process called "identify-investigate-arrest." Unless you are caught in a raid that targets someone else, or the police arrest and turn you over, the only way ICE will arrest you is by identifying and investigating you. Here is how they do that:

IDENTIFY: ICE identifies you from their database of undocumented people. There are approximately 540,000 people in their database of people with deportation orders. It's not known how they identify specific people over others. We do know that under President Obama, ICE was directed to go after the most dangerous. Under Trump, they go after everyone. It's assumed that they go after the easiest to locate.

INVESTIGATE: ICE has thousands of agents around the country whose job is to research and locate undocumented people. They use a variety of tactics to do that. Finding people today is much different from only ten years ago. Today, most of it is done with computers and technology rather than sneaking through neighborhoods. People leave **digital trails** which ICE uses to locate them. A digital trail is when you make any kind of electronic transaction using your name.

Examples of digital trails ICE can follow:
- ✓ You use Western Union to wire money to a family member in your home country
- ✓ You receive a traffic ticket and are put into the local database by the police
- ✓ The local police arrest you for any crime
- ✓ You register your car in certain states that work with ICE
- ✓ Your name is on Facebook or other social media sites
- ✓ A hotel that has an agreement with ICE turns over its registration lists
- ✓ You use a cell phone in your name that can be traced using cell phone towers
- ✓ Your name is in a court database after being charged with a crime

ICE investigators use a software called **Palantir** to combine all the known information about you. The database may give them a map of where you work, live, and go every day. From this, they can make their plan to arrest you.

ARREST: Usually done in the morning, a team of four or more ICE agents will arrive and use various tactics to gain entrance to your home and attempt to arrest and detain you. Former President Obama directed ICE to go after the worst criminals. Trump is directing ICE to go after all undocumented people.

ICE does not conduct random raids on individuals or neighborhoods. They do not walk the streets asking people to prove they are in the country legally. Every ICE raid happens because they have a warrant to arrest an undocumented person. But, they WILL arrest everyone at the raid who cannot prove they are in the country legally.

Tricks ICE May Use

ICE will not disclose all the tricks they use to arrest people. Below is a consolidation of tricks we found from various sources. Some ICE agents see catching you as a game. They will try to trick you into giving yourself up so they can arrest you.

Don't be fooled by these tricks:

- ✓ **Friend or family text:** ICE agents go to your house. You are not home, but some of your relatives are. An ICE agent takes your relative or friend's cellphone and sends you a text message. Pretending to be someone you know, they suggest that you meet somewhere. You receive the text message. Not realizing it is coming from an ICE agent, you go to the meeting place only to find agents waiting to arrest you.

- ✓ **Phone calls:** If they have your phone number, an ICE agent will call you, identify themselves, and request information such as where you were born and what your immigration status is. The ICE agent will say, "President Trump is considering changing immigration procedures, and if you turn yourself in early, we will give you a break." You should ignore these calls. If you receive calls from people you don't know, they are a scam or an ICE agent trying to trick you.

✓ **Pretending to be local police:**

a) An ICE agent comes to your door and yells "Police!" to get you to open the door. You might think something is happening in the neighborhood, but in fact, it is ICE trying to get you to open the door. Only open the door if you have a security chain or two that can prevent ICE from opening it further. Unless they have a warrant signed by a judge with your name and address on it, they have no right to enter your home. If it's ICE, close the door and ignore them. As soon as possible, call your Immigration Expert.

b) An ICE agent knocks on your door. However, they have covered up the words "ICE" on their clothing, so all that is exposed is the word "police." They ask about a stolen car and need evidence of who owns the vehicle in the driveway. You walk out to prove you are the owner. Then the ICE agent reveals themselves and arrests you. Before you open the door, ask them if they are local police or ICE. By law, they must answer. The best option is still to ignore them when they knock on your door.

c) An ICE agent knocks on your door and asks you to look at a photograph of a criminal suspect. They use the person's name they are looking for, but the picture is of a different person. You automatically correct the "error." The ICE agent asks to see the person to fix the "mistake." When they see the person they are looking for, they make the arrest. Don't be fooled.

d) Someone calls and informs you that you may be a victim of identity theft and they need to meet with you, or they describe your vehicle and say that someone claimed it was in an accident, so they need to stop by and inspect it. They arrive at your home, confirm your identity, and arrest you. It is safer to make yourself unavailable and have a legal resident talk to them or ignore them completely.

✓ **Motels:** ICE has been working with motels and hotels in Arizona, Washington, and other states to obtain their registration lists. They compare those lists to their database of known undocumented people. If they find a match, they send ICE agents to the motel to arrest you. If you stay at a motel, pay only with cash and change a few letters in your name so you are not detected in the ICE databases.

✓ **Jails:** As part of the 287(g) program, ICE works with the local police and has them compare the names of anyone they suspect to be undocumented with ICE databases. If the police arrest you and suspect you are undocumented, they will put your information into their database and you could be on your way to detention.

✓ **Courthouses:** Court hearings are public record. If you go to court for any reason, ICE can compare your name with their database. If they find a match, they will send agents to the court to pick you up. They are usually dressed in plain clothes and wait for you in the hallway.

✓ **License plate cameras:** ICE now has access to billions of license plate images that are captured by thousands of cameras around the country. When they find a match, they know where you live. From there they will use other techniques to find you. Most of these records are old. Buying a new license plate with a different number would be smart.

✓ **Social media:** One of the newest tricks is to find you on any of the social media sites which include Facebook, Instagram, Twitter, Tumblr, Weibo, Reddit, Flickr, LinkedIn, YouTube, Pinterest, Meetup, Sonico, MiGente, and more. ICE tracks these and many other sites, and they use programs to compare the people they are looking for with people on these sites. They use facial recognition software to compare pictures they have with faces on these sites to identify where people live and how to find them. The safest option is not to be on these sites. But if you must, use a slightly different name and minimize the use of your photo.

If you were given an "**A-Number**" at any time and you did not follow up on a court hearing or a required meeting with Immigration Services, you are likely on the ICE list. Call: 1-800-898-7180 and enter your A-Number to find out if you have a deportation order or to learn the latest information on your court case.

The secret to avoiding ICE is to go "off-grid." It means you should minimize your digital trail and avoid electronic transactions and internet interactions. If you know there is a deportation order out for you, you want to change how you live and work.

Here are some tips on how to avoid ICE:

Remember

✓ Find a new place to live without your name on the lease. Do not have mail sent to the new home. There should be no public record of you living there.

✓ Do not use credit cards. Pay cash for everything. Do not make any electronic transactions using your name.

✓ Be sure your car is not in your name or you have replaced your license plate in the last three years.

✓ If you are on social media such as Facebook, delete your account or use a different name and no photos of you.

✓ If someone sends you a text message that seems a little strange, call them. If they don't answer, then send a text saying you are not available now.

✓ Know the tricks that ICE uses and don't let them fool you.

✓ If you have family members who are documented, put everything in their names.

Summary of Tips: When walking, driving, working, associating with others, or even being at home:

✓ Be aware of who and what is around so you can notice anything unusual.

✓ Don't make changes to your car that might attract attention.

✓ Consider tinting your car windows.

✓ Be aware if anyone is following you on foot or in a car.

✓ Only carry your ID if you need it, and do not carry fake IDs.

✓ Don't carry anything that could be a weapon.

✓ Don't tell authorities where you are from, but also don't lie. Instead, stay silent.

✓ Demand to see your lawyer if you are arrested, and don't sign anything.

✓ Don't talk to strangers in your neighborhood who ask about people you know.

✓ Keep the doors in your house and vehicle locked.

✓ Don't open a door unless you are certain about who is on the other side.

✓ Consider installing a peephole and security chains on your door.

✓ Be aware of who you associate with; you don't want to end up in the wrong photo.

✓ Be careful of wearing gang-related items or making gang-related signs even as a joke.

✓ Think before you post anything on social media.

✓ Don't visit people who have an immigration warrant for their arrest (let them visit you).

✓ Do checks on your friends and family to know who is at risk.

Remember

Warning

Do this

Memorize

Laying low is important while you work on your documentation. Once your documents are submitted to Immigration Services and you have your receipt notice, you are safer. It is nearly impossible to get your paperwork done while in detention. During this time with Trump, you must be extra careful. If you follow our suggestions and stay aware of what is around you, you can get through this.

<u>Chapter Ten</u>

Working in the United States: Your Rights

"Mr. Speaker, our Nation depends on immigrants' labor, and I hope we can create an immigration system as dependable as they are."
–Luis Gutierrez

What You Will Learn:
- ✓ Your rights as an undocumented employee
- ✓ The E-Verify background check
- ✓ Work discrimination

Words to Know:

Workers' Compensation Insurance: The law requires all employers to carry this special insurance that pays for any injury while on the job. This insurance must cover all employees and contractors. Formerly called "workman's comp."

Employee Rights

Some employers take advantage of undocumented immigrants. However, all workers — documented or not — have workers' rights in the United States. While many employers get away with it, many others have gone to jail for violating workers' rights. **When it comes to employment rights, an undocumented person has almost the same rights as a legal citizen.** Employers cannot discriminate against you based on a physical problem, where you came from, your religion, age, or sex. However, it is against the law in the United States to hire an undocumented person. Employers find it tempting to hire you because they know you are willing to do work that U.S. citizens are not willing to do and that you may be willing to work for less. There is another law that if they do hire you anyway, they cannot simply fire you because you are undocumented. They must use another reason.

There are other laws that employers must follow as well. By law, employers should be taking taxes out of your pay. Employers should also pay you "overtime" if you work more than 40 hours a week. **If you work more than 40 hours in a week, you must be paid 1.5 times your normal rate for each hour over 40 hours. That is the law in the United States.** If you are paid by the piece, such as by the basket or bushel, they must still pay you the minimum wage plus overtime. However, if you are an agricultural worker, your employer is only required to pay the minimum wage and not overtime.

In the United States in 2018, the minimum wage is $7.25 an hour. Some cities and states have a higher minimum wage. For example, in the city of Seattle, the minimum wage is $15 an hour. In the state of Colorado, the minimum wage is $10.20 an hour. The hourly minimum wage is lower for workers who receive tips in addition to their employer-paid hourly wage, such as at restaurant employees.

Workers' Compensation

As an employee, your employer pays workers' compensation. It is a special insurance that will cover your expenses if you are injured on the job. Every employer is required to have compensation insurance for employees, documented or not. They may not pay for you to be off work healing, but legally they must keep your position available to you so you can go back to work after you have healed. They cannot force you to work if the doctor gives you a note that says you need to rest until you have healed. The doctor will provide a paper stating how long you need to rest.

If your employer threatens your job or forces you to work when you are injured, they are violating your rights. A poster of Employee Rights in English and Spanish must, by law, be on the wall in the company lunchroom or near the timeclock for you to read. If it's not there, seek out the hiring department for a copy. In each state, these laws may be slightly different.

If your employer is violating your rights, contact your Immigration Expert and ask for a referral to a lawyer who specializes in employee rights.

E-Verify Background Check

The United States government created a program called E-Verify that helps employers identify fake Social Security cards. Generally, within a few minutes, the employer can determine if a Social Security card is not real and accept or reject you. However, because states establish most employment laws, a state can decide if they require employers within that state to use the program. States that require all private employers to use E-Verify include:

- ✓ Alabama
- ✓ Arizona

✓ Georgia (for companies with more than 500 employees)
✓ Tennessee
✓ South Carolina
✓ North Carolina
✓ Mississippi
✓ Utah

There are other states with variations of the law. In these states, private companies are not required to use **E-Verify**, but government agencies or certain contractors may be required. Refer to a website in the *Useful Websites and Phone Numbers* part of this book that will give you a map of the laws in each state.

While the purpose of E-Verify is to reduce the number of undocumented workers in the United States, most employers ignore the program. A recent study found that even in states like Arizona that require verification, only 50% of the employers do the check. It seems that employers are willing to take the risk of hiring undocumented people because they are reliable. If you are rejected from a job because you failed E-Verify, it's likely another employer down the street is willing to take the chance if they think you are reliable.

Work Discrimination
Discrimination comes in many forms. Discrimination means an employer refuses to provide you an opportunity or service because of who you are (where you came from, the color of your skin, a physical issue, your religion, sex, or age). Discrimination could occur when looking for work, working at a job, renting or purchasing a home, or obtaining credit, for example. Discrimination in the United States is often because of the color of your skin.

An employer is discriminating against you if they:
✓ Ask for more documents from you than others to

complete your I-9 employment eligibility form
- ✓ Say they only hire U.S. citizens even if you have a green card or work permit
- ✓ Fire you for lying about your undocumented status (they cannot legally fire you for this)
- ✓ Offer you less than minimum wage
- ✓ Pay you less than other people for the same job because you are undocumented

If this discrimination ever happens to you, contact your Immigration Expert and ask them for a referral to a workers' compensation lawyer. You can file a complaint with the lawyer and possibly collect money through a lawsuit. If you don't have an Immigration Expert, contact a local non-profit immigration organization and ask them for a referral.

Tips to Remember:
- ✓ By law, your employer must pay you the minimum wage of $7.25 an hour (with exceptions in tipped jobs).
- ✓ By law, your employer must pay you the minimum wage up to 40 hours a week, and 1.5 times the minimum wage for overtime (when you work over 40 hours). There are some exceptions such as agricultural and contract labor.
- ✓ If you get hurt on the job, your employer must have workers' compensation insurance that covers the cost of your injury.
- ✓ Your employer cannot fire you if they discover you are undocumented.
- ✓ If you are turned down for a job because E-Verify found a problem with your Social Security number, find another potential employer.

<u>Conclusion</u>

Making This Book Better

"The biggest room in the world is the room for improvement."
–Helmut Schmidt

We like this quote because it represents our book. While we believe we have researched and written the most comprehensive book for immigrants to date, there is room for improvement. And that is where you come in. The last chapter is about helping us make it better. The greatest challenge with immigration law is that it's constantly changing and so are the tactics used to detain and deport you.

We started this project over a year ago from a conversation with a new client who walked into the office. She had spent over $8,500 and three years with a lawyer and had nothing for the investment. She had no idea what the lawyer was doing for her, what her status was, or what her chances were. We also spent many evenings at our favorite Mexican Restaurant in Colorado and gained the confidence of the employees. They told us frightful stories of ICE driving up and down the streets of their community only to scare them. They told us how people have retreated into their homes to hide. To us, it was reminiscent of Nazi Germany in 1938. We thought there needed to be a book about immigration written in everyday language for the average person. This book would help people understand the immigration process enough to ask questions and offer ideas when speaking with an Immigration Expert.

The rest of the book was written to help you understand how

to survive these difficult times until a sense of sanity returns to our government.

As we did our research, we realized that immigration law is what one lawyer called a "Japanese paper fan." Each way you open it, it looks a little different. That is the truth about everyone's case in immigration. To make the process more difficult, what worked last year in immigration law may not work this year. While we wrote this book, it became a daily routine to read all the latest news articles and immigration announcements. Often, we would have to go back and rewrite sections to keep it up to date. As we write this today, a judge blocked Trump's attempt to end DACA. He gave Trump 90 days to write a justifiable reason for ending DACA or to open the program up to new entrants. Another judge blocked Trump's desire to keep immigrants and their families in concentration camps until their case was concluded. We shall see.

Every four to six months we will update this book. We will make the most important updates available on our blog posts at:

HTTPS://migrationresearchers.wordpress.com

Meanwhile, learn to lay low, and let's get through this until the government establishes sensible immigration laws.

WE WANT YOUR STORIES

We want your feedback. Please write to us in English or Spanish and tell us your story. If we use your story, we will not use your last name or location. We will keep personal details confidential.

Please write to us and give us your experiences either on our blog or by letter. Let's all work together to make this book better for everyone. We want to make America even greater than it has been. Specifically, we are looking for the following:

✓ Did you or someone you know have an encounter in which ICE violated your rights? Tell us your story. We may include it on our blog or in the book update. Your experience could help others know what to do.

✓ If you or someone you know had an encounter with ICE, what did the agents do? Do you have a story you can share about a trick they played?

✓ If you were in detention, how were you treated? Lawyers are suing detention centers over the mistreatment of people. What was the judge like? If anyone did not treat you fairly, tell us about it.

✓ Were you the victim of a scam? Did someone trick you and cause you to lose money? What was their scam? Tell us your story so we can tell it again and help others to not fall into the same trap.

✓ Did an immigration lawyer or a notary take your money and not do anything to help you? What was their trick? What did they say to you?

✓ Has a judge treated you unfairly? If so, what was the judge's name and what was said or done to you?

Remember, if you were the victim of a crime committed by anyone, and that includes ICE, police, judges, lawyers, and other officials, you could qualify for a U-Visa.

If you have any stories about your experience with Immigration Services, police, ICE, lawyers, employers, or anything else that may be useful for upcoming editions of the book, please write to us.

Final Comments

Former President Ronald Reagan is quoted as saying, *"I received a letter just before I left office from a man. I don't know why he chose to write it, but I'm glad he did. He wrote that you can go to live in France, but you can't become a Frenchman. You can go to live in Germany or Italy, but you can't become a German, or Italian. He went through Turkey, Greece, Japan and other countries. But he said anyone, from any corner of the world, can come to live in the United States and become an American."*

What makes the United States great are the immigrants who come here risking everything for a better, safer life. The United States is great today because we can dream, and if we work hard, succeed. It's our success which makes America Great. The era of Trump will come and go. Meanwhile, we hope you will still be here working on your immigration papers or having become documented. And, we hope you will continue to contribute to the success of the United States and continue to make the United States even greater.

Migration Research LLC
P.O. Box 941
Flagstaff Arizona 86002-0941

Email: **info@migration-research.com**
Blog: **https://migrationresearchers.wordpress.com**

Common Questions and Answers about Immigration

Introduction

Incorporating information from the U.S. Citizenship and Immigration Services website (**https://www.uscis.gov**), we have compiled a list of the most common immigration questions. We have simplified the wording so that everyone can understand the meanings. Keep in mind that only an authorized Immigration Expert can provide legal advice, as every immigration case is different.

Can I travel while being undocumented?

If you have valid identification (ID) such as a passport from any country, it is safe to travel by airplane, train, or bus in the United States UNLESS you are within **100 miles** of the border. Areas within 100 miles of the border have numerous ID checks. It is also risky to fly if your airplane takes you out of the country. If you travel, do not keep any fake documents on you.

Can I travel while I am in immigration proceedings?

Yes, you can travel anywhere in the country with a valid ID, such as a passport. You should keep a copy of your most recent Immigration Services letter with you. Children under the age of 18 do not need IDs. You cannot leave the United States until you have obtained permanent residency status (a green card). Remember, you must not miss any court dates. If you do travel, keep the time away from home to a minimum until you have obtained your status.

Can I still apply for asylum even if I am in the United States illegally?

Yes. You may apply for asylum regardless of your immigration status. If you are in removal proceedings, you will have the chance to apply for Defensive Asylum, **CAT,** or Withholding of Removal. See *Chapter Three*.

If you are not in removal proceedings, you can still apply for Affirmative Asylum. If you missed the one-year deadline to apply, you can still qualify if you have a good reason for missing it. For example:

- ✓ You were traumatized by what happened to you in your home country.
- ✓ You were included on another application, but it was denied.
- ✓ You hired a lawyer, but they failed to complete your application on time.

How can minor criminal offenses affect my application?

In Trump's America, virtually ANY offense can get you deported. ICE will deport you unless you can qualify for staying by explaining that you were the victim of a crime in the United States, or that you fear for your life if returned to your home country. If you have any convictions, contact an Immigration Expert to find a way to reduce or eliminate the charges. A **Supreme Court** decision in April of 2018 has made it more difficult to deport you on minor crimes.

What if I do not notify Immigration Services of my change of address when I move?

With Trump, there is little or no forgiveness. Miss a court date, and you will be issued a Failure to Appear letter. It will turn into an automatic notice of deportation which will terminate your case. When in proceedings, keep your address up to date.

Your Immigration Expert can do that for you, or you can do it yourself. You need to print out the form "**AR-11** Change of Address" from the internet and mail it or submit it online. If you are in court proceedings, you must also inform the court of your change of address. You must personally go to the local court and fill out the paper for a change of address. You must make a copy of this document and send it to the Office of Chief Counsel: ICE. Your local court will tell you how.

I have an outstanding removal and deportation order. Should I ignore it?

That depends on you. If you voluntarily leave the country, you can apply for legal status in the future. However, if you do not leave by the date on the letter and you get detained, you could be barred for ten or more years.

What happens if I sneak back into the U.S. after being deported?

If you are caught, ICE will immediately deport you unless you can convince officials that your life will be in danger if you are returned to your home country. If you cannot convince them, you will be deported and permanently barred from re-entering.

Can I apply for a green card if I am in the United States on a work visa?

You can only apply through **Marriage Petition** (you marry a U.S. citizen), **Family Petition** (your citizen/resident parent, spouse, or child petitions for you), or Asylum Application (you fear you will be harmed or killed if deported). In some circumstances, your employer can petition for you if you have skills not found with U.S. citizen workers. See *Chapter Three*.

Can I include my spouse and children in my application (Asylum, U-Visa, or VAWA)? Yes, you can. If you claim asylum or you applied for a U-Visa, you may include your

unmarried children or spouse. If you are a minor, you can also include your parents (U-Visa). If you filed a petition for a VAWA, you can include your unmarried children. If any of your children are victims of abuse, you can include all of them in your VAWA application. See *Chapter Three*.

What happens to the money I paid into Social Security while I was undocumented?

Unfortunately, you cannot claim any of the money you put into Social Security while using a false number.

If I am undocumented, why would I need an Individual Taxpayer Identification Number (ITIN)?

An ITIN will help you receive a tax refund for taxes you paid to the government. It may also provide you with tax credits for your children who are under the age of 18 and currently living with you. Having tax returns also proves "good moral character" for immigration purposes.

Can I move to a different state while being in court proceedings?

It is not wise to move to a new state while in court proceedings. But if you decide to move, you have two options:

1) Travel back and forth: You can move but continue your proceedings by attending hearings and interviews in the former state by traveling back and forth. However, that can be time-consuming and expensive. Inform Immigration Services and the court of your new address change.

2) Request a Change of Venue: This is a written approval by the judge to transfer your case to a court in your new state. An Immigration Expert can do this but will charge you up to $1500. To save money, go to the court in your old state and ask for a **Motion to Change Venue form.** Complete this form with a written statement of why you want to change venues, such as

that you have family members or job opportunities in the new state, for example. Submit the form and your statement to your old court and send a copy to the Office of Chief Counsel: ICE in your old state. You'll receive a notification granting or denying your request. If you plan on moving, complete this request as soon as possible.

Disadvantages of a Change of Venue:

✓ You will receive a new court date that might be delayed by a year or more.

✓ If you have only recently filed your Asylum Application and you are waiting for the 180 days to pass before being eligible for a work permit, the 180-day clock stops when the judge grants the motion to change venue. The clock starts again at your next hearing date in the new state. It will delay your work permit.

If I have already filed an Asylum Application, can I add my spouse and children later?

Doing so would slow the process, as your **180-day clock** would stop and set to zero until your next hearing. Any changes will stop and reset your clock. If you have already reached the required 180 days or you have already filed or received your EAD card, then you can add your spouse or children without delay.

How can I find out if I have reached the necessary 180 days?

✓ If you are in court proceedings: Call the court case hotline at **1-800-898-7180** and follow the instructions in English or Spanish. It is an automated system with all kinds of information including your 180-day clock.

✓ If you are applying for Affirmative Asylum: You or your Immigration Expert will receive a receipt notice from Immigration Services. The date of receipt is on the notice. From this date on you count 150 days. At that point, you can submit your application for your EAD card. Remember, after 150 days you can apply for your work permit. After 180 days you are eligible for work.

Can I change my Immigration Expert while being in court proceedings?

Yes, you can, but it will cost you time and money. Your new Immigration Expert will have to file a Motion to Substitute Counsel, or your former lawyer will have to file a Motion to Withdraw. Your new Immigration Expert will need access to your file. Make sure to keep a copy of your file. If you do not have it, request a copy from your old Immigration Expert.

What happens if my asylum claim gets denied at the Affirmative Asylum interview?

If you disagree with the denial, Immigration Services transfers your case to an immigration judge. You will receive a court hearing date and a second chance to prove your case in court. If the immigration judge denies your application, you can appeal three more times in higher courts. The process can take three or four years. Meanwhile, you can work in the United States. You should have an Immigration Expert for all proceedings as this is complicated and expensive. It will buy you time, and laws on immigration can change as President Trump will not be around forever. Another option is voluntary departure.

After the judge denies your application, you can sign a **voluntary departure** form. Immigration Services will give you 60-120 days to prepare for your departure. Because you have no Order of Removal on your record, you can re-apply in the future.

Can I be deported before filing an appeal on a denied asylum case?

You will have 30 days to file an appeal of this decision. If you miss the deadline, you are subject to deportation.

Deferred Action for Childhood Arrival (DACA) Common Questions and Answers

If Immigration Services approved my application under DACA, am I eligible for employment authorization?
Yes. Under existing regulations, if you received a deferred notice, you may obtain employment authorization from Immigration Services.

Under President Trump, can I renew my DACA and employment authorization?
Yes. You may request a renewal of your DACA status. Immigration Services reviews requests on a case-by-case basis. If they renew your case, you will receive Deferred Action status for another two years, and you will most likely receive a work permit for that period as well.

With DACA status, will I be able to travel outside of the United States?
No. At this time, the Trump government has cancelled any Advanced Parole for DACA recipients.

If convicted of a felony, a serious misdemeanor offense, or multiple misdemeanors, will I lose my DACA status?
Yes. If convicted of a felony offense, a significant misdemeanor offense, or three or more other misdemeanor offenses not occurring on the same date and not arising out of the same act, omission, or scheme of misconduct, you will lose your status and likely be deported.

What will happen to the information on DACA applications?
Immigration Services has a policy that they will not share information about a DACA applicant or applicant's family

members with ICE unless the person has committed a serious crime.

If Trump successfully terminates the DACA program, will I be deported?
The DACA program is unlikely to be terminated because three separate courts have concluded that his plan to do so is not constitutional. That means only the Supreme Court or Congress can decide. However, even if the program were to end, DACA recipients would most likely not be deported quickly because that would attract bad media attention and would distract from the need to focus attention on people who have committed real crimes.

Temporary Protected Status (TPS) Common Questions and Answers

If I get TPS, can I travel in and out of the country?
Yes, if you follow the rules carefully. If you originally arrived without documentation, leaving and re-entering with certain documents can help you. Read about TPS in *Chapter Two*.
You can use Advanced Parole and the Application for Travel Document (form **I-131**) to leave the country and then re-enter. A re-entry is considered a legal entry. This can help later in a Family Petition.

I have TPS. Can I apply for my relatives to come to the U.S.?
No, having TPS will not allow you to bring in family members. You would have to be a Green Card Holder, and as one, you could only bring in your direct relatives (spouse and children).

With TPS, how long will my work permit be good?
Once you receive TPS, you can also receive an Employment Authorization Document (EAD). It will expire at the same time as your TPS. Immigration Services will automatically extend it for six months when the president announces the renewal of the TPS program for your country. If your employer questions your status, ask your Immigration Expert for a copy of the country extension along with the six-month notice. Or, you can download it from the internet. We have provided a link in the *Useful Websites and Phone Numbers* part of this book.

If I am granted TPS and can legally work for a U.S. employer, can that employer sponsor me for a green card?
Yes, but it depends on the job. The process can be long, difficult, and expensive. The approval comes down to your level of education and unique skills. You must obtain a Labor

Certification to prove that no U.S. citizen has the skills to do the job you do.

If Immigration Services denies my TPS application, can I appeal?

Yes, unless your case was denied because of a felony or other national security issue. To appeal, you would file a Motion to Reconsider (I-290B). However, don't try to do an appeal on your own. You need an Immigration Expert to help you on this.

Meanings of Common Legal Words

When dealing with legal issues, it is common to hear certain words that you do not understand. Here are several legal terms you may hear from your Immigration Expert, in notices, or in court.

Adjudicate/Adjudication: To make a formal decision on a case. Immigration Services's review of your application to determine if you are eligible for that immigration benefit.

Admissibility: The process to determine if you can legally enter the United States.

Alien: Any person who is not a citizen of the United States. An Alien is any person living in the United States that does not have a United States passport. It includes Green Card Holders.

Alien Registration Number (A-Number): A unique seven-, eight-, or nine-digit number assigned to you by the Department of Homeland Security.

Asylee: A foreign national living in the United States or arrives at a port of entry which is unwilling to return to their country of birth and wishing to seek the protection because of fear of persecution based on religion, nationality, membership in a particular social group or political opinion.

Beneficiary: An immigrant who is sponsored by a relative or a business. A "principal beneficiary" is an immigrant named on an immigrant or nonimmigrant application. A "derivative beneficiary" is an immediate family member of the principal beneficiary.

Biometrics: The processes used to identify people based on their physical traits, including fingerprints, eye scan, photograph, and signature.

Burden of Proof: The requirement to present evidence to support a claim you have made. For example, if you claim you would be harmed if returned to your home country, the court may require you to prove that claim.

CBP: An abbreviation for U.S. Customs and Border Protection, an agency within the Department of Homeland Security. They are also known as the border guards.

Conditional Resident: Any immigrant granted permanent resident status on a conditional basis. For example, if you married a U.S. citizen or Green Card Holder and received a green card, your status will be "conditional" for two years. If you have maintained the relationship for that period, you can apply for Permanent Resident status.

Continuous Residence: The length of time you have maintained a permanent home in the United States after being admitted as a lawful permanent resident.

Credible Story: A story or explanation that demonstrates the person has a credible fear of returning to their home country and will be harmed or killed if deported.

DACA: An abbreviation for Deferred Action for Childhood Arrivals, a program launched in 2012. It temporally protects people who were brought to the United States by their parents when they were children.

Deferred Action: A type of prosecutorial discretion that allows an individual to remain in the United States for a set period unless it is terminated for some reason. DACA is a form of deferred action established by Former President Obama.

Department of Homeland Security (DHS): Department of the executive branch of the U.S. government charged with homeland security.

Department of Justice (DOJ): Part of the United States government with the responsibility to seek punishment for those guilty of illegal actions.

Discrimination: Unfair treatment in the workplace because of your race, color, religion, sex (including pregnancy), citizenship or immigration status, national origin, disability, or age.

Domestic worker: Individuals who take care of children, clean the house, or do upkeep of a home or surrounding yard on a regular basis in return for wages or other benefits, and who are not independent contractors.

F-1 Nonimmigrant Student: A person admitted to the United States as a full-time academic student at an accredited college.

Field Office: Offices within a **USCIS** district that provide services and enforcement functions.

Foreign National: A person without U.S. citizenship or nationality.

I-94: Arrival/Departure document.

ICE: An abbreviation for Immigration and Customs Enforcement, an agency of the Department of Homeland Security.

INA: An abbreviation for the Immigration and Nationality Act.

Inadmissibility: Not being allowed to legally enter the United States or obtain a visa based on past acts or conduct.

IRS: The Internal Revenue Services. A division of the United States government whose job it is to collect taxes and issue refunds.

ITIN: Individual Taxpayer Identification Number. Allows people without a Social Security number to pay taxes. Issued by the IRS, the tax division of the United States Government.

Jurisdiction: A designated area established by the government to govern and enforce laws.

Lawful Permanent Resident (LPR): Any person who is living in the U.S. legally but who is not a citizen of the United States. Also known as "permanent resident alien," "resident alien permit holder," and "Green Card Holder."

Parole: The discretionary decision that allows certain immigrants to leave an inspection facility and live in the United States under certain conditions.

Permanent Resident Card (Form I-551): Also known as a green card or alien registration card, this card is issued to immigrants as evidence of their legal status in the United States.

Probable Cause: A reasonable basis for believing that a crime may have been or is being committed. For example, if you drive up to a border inspection station with a car that has a strong odor of marijuana coming from it, officers will have probable cause to suspect you are transporting an illegal substance.

Port of Entry: Any location along an international border designated as an inspection point. All district offices and service centers are also considered ports because they are locations of entry for immigrants adjusting their immigrant status.

Pro-Bono: At no cost; free. A practicing lawyer who decides to take on a case at no charge.

Prosecutorial Discretion: The legal authority to choose whether to take action against an individual for committing an offense.

Provisional Unlawful Presence Waiver (I-601A): Waiver for individuals who are otherwise inadmissible, but are allowed to stay in the United States based on demonstrating **extreme hardship** to certain U.S. citizen or lawful permanent resident family members. The waiver allows the individual to return to the United States after departure for an immigrant visa interview at a U.S. embassy or consulate.

Refugee: Generally, any person outside his or her country of nationality who is unable or unwilling to return to that country because of persecution or a well-founded fear of persecution.

Regulations: Rules issued by a government authority to carry out the rule of law.

Reject (as compared to denial): When Immigration Services determines that an application cannot be accepted for intake and processing because it lacks a basic requirement (for example, a required fee or signature).

Removal: The deportation of an alien from the United States.

Temporary Protected Status (TPS): A temporary condition applied to certain people living in or visiting the United States due to conditions in their country that prevent them from returning safely.

UAC: Unaccompanied Alien Child: A person under the age of 18 who enters the U.S. without parents or legal guardians.

U.S. Citizenship and Immigration Services (USCIS): A federal agency in the Department of Homeland Security that oversees lawful immigration to the United States.

U.S. Customs and Border Protection (CBP): An agency of the Department of Homeland Security that is responsible for preventing the illegal entry of people and products while allowing legal travel and trade.

U.S. Immigration and Customs Enforcement (ICE): An arm of the U.S. Department of Homeland Security whose job it is to enforce federal laws governing border control, trade, and immigration.

USCIS Number: Same as an "**A-Number**." A unique, 9-digit number assigned to a noncitizen by the Department of Homeland Security. It is on the front of Permanent Resident Cards.

Visa: Most visas are inserted in a person's passport. It allows them to enter the United States under certain conditions.

Willful Misrepresentation: Knowingly making a statement or a claim that is not fully true or factual; lying.

Useful Websites and Phone Numbers

We wrote this book to minimize the need for using the internet. However, for those who would like to learn more about becoming documented beyond what this book offers, here is a list of our favorite websites with a short description of how they can help you. We have also included useful phone numbers.

For children who made it across the border without their parents and are still under the age of 18. **Unaccompanied Children Resource Center: https://www.uacresources.org/**

What happens in **immigration court** and how to respond during your individual hearing: **https://www.youtube.com/watch?v=bj26uKz74cc**

A national organization that will help you **find a lawyer** who has a good reputation: **http://www.ailalawyer.com/**

An updated list of **police departments that work with ICE: https://www.ice.gov/287g**

This government site will tell you the **status of a person**. You must know their A-Number or their name, country of birth, and birth date: **https://locator.ice.gov/**

States that will issue **driver licenses** to certain undocumented people: **http://www.ncsl.org/research/immigration/states-offering-driver-s-licenses-to-immigrants.aspx**

IRS website for the **W-7 ITIN** form: **https://www.irs.gov/pub/irs-pdf/fw7.pdf**

The United States Government has a list of **free and low-cost immigration lawyers by state**: **www.justice.gov/eoir/list-pro-bono-legal-service-providers-map**

A website that helps people find the closest **non-profit immigration services office**: **https://www.immigrationadvocates.org/nonprofit/legaldirectory/**

A great resource that offers additional information about your rights and **how to find a lawyer** you can trust: **https://www.informedimmigrant.com**

Map of states with various **E-Verify laws**: **http://www.trackercorp.com/everify-legislation-map.php**

A government website that provides the latest information on **your country's TPS designation**. Select the tab Countries Currently Designated for TPS: **https://www.uscis.gov/humanitarian/temporary-protected-status**

The largest **national Hispanic civil rights organization**: **http://www.nclr.org/**

United We Dream is the **largest youth site for undocumented and DACA immigrants**. You will find information on how to be prepared and how to become legal: **https://unitedwedream.org/**

Learn what are the **odds of the Judge appointed to your case granting your petition**: **https://www.reuters.com/investigates/special-report/usa-immigration-asylum/**

IMMIGRATION CONTACT INFORMATION FOR USCIS
1-800-375-5283

U.S. Citizenship and Immigration Services (**USCIS**) provides a phone number that you can use to learn about several issues regarding your immigration status. The information is provided in both English and Spanish. It is mostly an automated service which means you do not speak to a person. However, people are available to help you with questions during certain hours. The automated part is available 24 hours a day. Before you call, have any papers you received from **USCIS** in front of you along with your receipt number (look for the number on your **USCIS** letter).

This service will allow you to:

✓ **Update your existing application:** Printed on the letter Immigration Services sent you is a receipt number. If you enter this, the recording will give you details such as your current status and the date of your next hearing.

✓ **Submit a change of address:** If you move while you are in immigration proceedings, it is extremely important to submit your new address to Immigration Services, so they know how to contact you for appointment notices. Lawyers will often charge you $50 to change your address. This phone service will allow you to do it for free. You will also have to notify your local court of your address change.

✓ **Find out immigration office locations:** If you recently moved, need to find a certain office, or are looking for the location of your biometrics appointment, this service can help you find the right place.

Automated Court Case Information Hotline
1-800-898-7180

Follow the instructions and enter your **A-Number**. The automated recording (available in English and Spanish) will tell you:

✓ The date, time, and location of your next hearing

✓ Any decisions issued by the immigration court

✓ The status or availability of appeals

✓ Other relevant deadlines

Qualifying Crimes Which Could Lead to a Green Card

Have you been the victim of any crime in the United States? Or, have you experienced abuse in your home country which would put your life in danger if you were deported?

If you have been the victim of any of the crimes or abuses listed below, you may qualify for the corresponding visas or statuses.

VAWA	U Visa	T Visa	SIJS	Asylum
Battery or extreme cruelty caused by a U.S. Citizen or LPR spouse or parent or an adult U.S. Citizen son or daughter	Rape, torture, trafficking, incest, Domestic violence, sexual assault, abusive sexual contact, prostitution, sexual exploitation, stalking, female genital mutilation, being held hostage, peonage, involuntary servitude, slave trade, kidnapping, abduction, false imprisonment, blackmail, extortion, manslaughter, murder, felonious assault, witness tampering, obstruction of justice, perjury, or fraud in foreign labor contracting	Sex or labor trafficking,\n\nSex trafficking requires element of force, fraud or coercion unless the sex trafficking survivor is under 18\n\nLabor trafficking includes recruitment harboring, transportation, provision, or obtaining of a person for labor or services, through use of force, fraud, or coercion for purposes of involuntary servitude, peonage, debt bondage or slavery	Parental abandonment, abuse, neglect, or a similar basis under state law (abandonment, abuse, neglect are defined by and evaluated under the relevant state law).\n\nNot in child's best interest to be returned to country of origin	Persecution or a well-founded fear of future persecution based on race, religion, nationality, membership in a particular social group, or political opinion

A Note from the Author,

I am an immigrant myself. I came to the U.S. in 2015 from Europe because I married a U.S. Citizen. We were married in the U.S. in 2014 and quickly realized that following the laws as they are written meant that I must return to Europe and go through the marriage petition process. Often immigration will look the other way when you marry while in the U.S. on a tourist visa; but doing so is also considered "visa-fraud." Rather than breaking any laws, we went to Germany and lived on our savings while we waited the nine-months it took to go through the process. It was expensive and difficult even though our case was considered simple. By comparison, it took a mere 30 days and 100 Euros for my husband to receive his European Green card.

My first experience in the U.S. was in the state of Colorado. Of all the jobs I could have taken, I ended up in immigration. I was lucky as I ended up working for one of the most experienced and talented immigration lawyers in the state. She was my mentor, and I was able to dive deep into the world of immigration. Most of our clients were from Latin America, India, Iraq, and Kenya. All were hardworking honest families who ran from their countries for fear of persecution. They were forced to leave their home, family, and friends. It's hard enough to start a new life in a new country. It's even harder when you don't speak the language or understand the system. Believe me, I know, and I speak the language.

As a child, I was taught about America in school. We learned about the "melting pot" of societies from around the world that made up this great country. The teacher said it is a country of immigrants and opportunities. Success comes to those willing to work hard and take chances. Written much later, but stories like "From Dishwasher to Millionaire" were examples of what we were taught.
I also learned about my history; one of Nazi Germany.

Concerningly, as time has gone on with this new Trump government, I have found it easy to compare what happened in my birth country. In Germany the war began with the Jews, here it begins with the Immigrants. In both places, the people began to rationalize hatred and discrimination to justify their tribalism.

Eighteen months ago, I arrived home one evening frustrated over several conversations I had with clients. Past lawyers they were working with left them with little information about their case and then charged them exorbitant fees. They would go home fearing that ICE was looking for them. My husband Andy assumed there was a book to help undocumented people answer simple questions. To his surprise there was not. Recognizing the need, a little over a year ago, we began writing this book.

It has been a long stressful journey of researching, writing and re-writing. To complicate things more Trumps people are continuously changing the rules requiring constant updates. Even as we publish this book, new changes are underway. We are committed to informing people of changes on our blog and to update this book every six months and possibly sooner.

I'm sure you know by now; this book does not teach you how to become documented, it teaches you how to be prepared, how to ask the right questions with your Immigration Expert, how not to be ripped off and how to avoid ICE in the meantime. We truly hope you get something out of it.

#####

For those reading this that are Citizens and LPR's who want to get involved: We have done the best possible job to write a book that is simple to understand. But even with this knowledge, navigating the immigration system is difficult. You can help:

✦ If you need someone that needs help, read this book and help explain their options.

Remember, you are NOT giving them advice. Only a lawyer can do that

+ Help them find a good immigration expert with the advice we offer
+ Read *Chapter Eight* and help them develop a plan
+ Review each chapter with their families
+ Find ways to spread the word through Meetups or church events. Teach everyone how to be prepared

To make America even greater than it is we must go forward, not to the times that once destroyed my country. America still is the melting pot of our world, let's keep it that way.

Sabine Wiesemeyer

Notes

Notes

Notes

www.ingramcontent.com/pod-product-compliance
Lightning Source LLC
Chambersburg PA
CBHW071255220526
45468CB00001B/140